PICTURE IT IN
COUNTED BEADWORK

PICTURE IT IN
COUNTED BEADWORK

GILLIAN LEEPER
CHRISTINE BARKER

David & Charles

Introduction

IN 1991 Gillian's business Spoilt for Choice began to specialise in embroidery beads, in particular using them in place of thread to produce designs on counted fabric. This was the birth of the successful Beadesign range of beads and kits based on the Victorian tradition of counted beadwork. My own fascination with beads led me to stitching samples for Gillian which, in turn, inspired me to produce my own designs. This book, which is a combination of our individual talents and personalities, came about through our long-standing friendship and mutual interest in needlework.

Beads have featured in many cultures over the centuries and have been used to denote status, adorn fabric and signify religion. The word bead comes from the Anglo-Saxon *bede* meaning a prayer and, over time, has come to refer to the beads themselves, on which prayers are counted.

In the 1800s, Berlin work became very popular and the Victorians often combined beads with yarn in their needlework. Counted beadwork, which is based on cross stitch, is a revival of this technique.

The aim of this book is to provide a comprehensive range of charts and patterns for counted beadwork. We hope that beginners, having mastered the basic techniques, will be encouraged to adapt these to suit their own requirements. Experienced embroiderers can also adapt their existing cross stitch charts to combine both techniques.

Where appropriate, we have suggested alternative ways of completing the designs, but these suggestions are by no means exhaustive and we hope the reader will enjoy going on to explore the many design possibilities provided by the myriad colours of beads available and, ultimately, to produce original pieces of work.

Christine Barker

Materials, Techniques and Stitches

Before starting work on a design you will need to assemble a few essential needlework items. Using the correct materials helps to produce a finished design that you will be proud of. As there is nothing more frustrating than finally sitting down to begin work only to discover that you do not have all the necessary equipment, make sure that you assemble everything, including suitable containers for your beads, before you begin.

FABRIC

Counted beadwork is usually worked, using size 11/0 beads (see page 115), on 14-count Aida fabric which is fabric woven especially for cross stitch. The count is particularly important in counted beadwork as a smaller number of blocks to 1 inch (25mm) causes gaps between the beads while a larger number will not allow sufficient space for the beads to lie correctly on the fabric. Smaller (size 14/0) beads should be sewn on to 18-count fabric (see page 118).

AIDA
This is a fine, cotton fabric with threads which are easy to count. It is readily available from needlework shops and comes in many colours and several finishes. It is woven to form blocks of threads with holes in-between, and one bead is sewn over one block. Most of the projects in this book are sewn on 14-count (14 holes to 1 inch (25mm) Aida.

Rustico Aida has a nubbed finish for a 'country' look. Damask Aida is a mixture of rayon and cotton and is softer and silkier than 100% cotton. The rayon content gives it a sheen and makes it perfect for stitchery for special occasions such as weddings or anniversaries. Aida needs careful handling as it frays easily. It is best to oversew the edges of the fabric before beginning to stitch, this will prevent fraying.

STITCHING/PERFORATED PAPER
The Victorians were particularly interested in working on perforated, or punched, paper and used it to make greetings cards, needlecases, bookmarks and other small items. Stitching/perforated paper is available in 14-count (14 holes to 1 inch (25mm), and in a variety of glorious colours. Beads sit particularly well on paper and, when the design is complete, the paper can be cut, glued or folded to produce interesting cards or gifts. Although it is fairly strong, it needs to be stitched with care as it can tear. It also has a 'right' and 'wrong' side. This is obvious on gold or silver paper as only the 'right' side is coloured but, with other colours, the 'right' side is the smoother side. To stitch beads on to paper, use two strands of thread for extra security.

PLASTIC CANVAS
Available in 14-count (14 holes to 1 inch (25mm), and in a variety of colours, plastic canvas can be used to make jewellery and items such as boxes. Beads should be attached with two strands of thread and the design should not be cut out until it is complete.

VINYL WEAVE
This is a 14-count vinyl fabric woven to look like Aida. It is available in white or cream. It does not fray and can be cut to any shape after the design

is complete. Vinyl weave is ideal for placemats, tray cloths and similar items as it can be sponged clean. For extra security, use two strands of thread to sew on the beads.

NEEDLES

'SHARPS'
A 'Sharps' size 10 needle is fine enough to pass easily through both the beads and the holes of the fabric, take care not to pierce or split the threads of the fabric with the point of the needle.

BEADING NEEDLES
These are fine, pliable needles with very small eyes and should be used to attach small (size 14/0) beads. They can also be used as an alternative to 'Sharps'.

TAPESTRY NEEDLES
For back stitch or cross stitch, use a tapestry needle, size 24 or 26. It is far easier to thread stranded cotton (embroidery floss) through a needle with a large eye and the blunt end helps to ensure that you do not split the threads of the fabric.

THREADS

POLYESTER SEWING THREAD
To attach the beads, use polyester sewing thread in a colour to match the background fabric. Use only short lengths of thread. Long threads can easily become knotted and are weakened as they pass through the fabric. You can wax the thread to make it stronger by pulling it over a tablet of beeswax until it is completely coated with wax. Waxing the thread also helps to prevent twists and knots. Beeswax is available from haberdashery departments.

EMBROIDERY THREAD (floss)
Where designs include cross stitch or back stitch, DMC or Madeira stranded cotton (embroidery floss) and DMC flower threads have been used. DMC flower thread is a beautiful, single-strand matt thread which gives a very smooth finish. It can be used in place of stranded cotton (embroidery floss).

On 14-count fabric use two strands of stranded cotton (embroidery floss) for cross stitch, for back

stitch where it outlines beads, and for letters or numbers. Where back stitch is used to outline cross stitch, use only one strand. To separate the strands, cut a length of thread not more than 12 inches (300mm). Separate all six strands and re-combine them as required.

BLENDING FILAMENT AND METALLIC THREAD
In some projects, Kreinik blending filament or DMC metallic threads have been used, either alone, or combined with stranded cotton (embroidery floss), to add sparkle to the design. These threads are available in a wide range of colours. Kreinik braid and cord are used alone, and give more definition than blending filament or metallic thread.

SCISSORS

Use dressmaking scissors for cutting fabric, and take care to follow the line of threads so that you have a straight edge. You will also need a pair of sharp embroidery scissors for snipping threads. Scissors with a hooked end are particularly useful for undoing mistakes without catching the fabric. Hang your scissors on a ribbon round your neck or tie them to a scissor-keeper to avoid losing them down the side of your chair.

EMBROIDERY HOOPS AND FRAMES

Using an embroidery hoop is a matter of personal preference. It will keep your fabric taut and your beadwork even, but you should use one only if

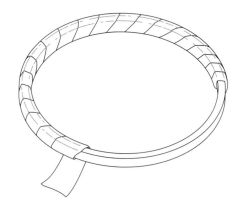

● *Binding the inner ring of an embroidery hoop with tape*

the whole design can be worked without being moved within the frame. If you try to re-position a hoop over existing beadwork the lie of the beads will be distorted, spoiling the finished effect of your work. Circular hoops are available in many sizes so it should be possible to find one to fit your design. If you bind the inner hoop with white bias tape, securing it with two or three back stitches, your fabric will not become damaged or slip when it is in the hoop.

Flexi-hoops are available from most craft shops and are useful for working some projects and then for framing the finished design. They are inexpensive and come in a variety of shapes, sizes and colours.

You may need to use a frame for those larger pieces of work that will not fit inside an embroidery hoop. Rectangular frames are available in many sizes. They consist of two wooden stretchers at the side, and two wooden rollers held together by wing-nuts. Webbing is nailed to each roller and the fabric is then attached to it. The fabric must not be any wider than the webbing, but it can be longer than the frame as any excess is wound on to the rollers when it is not being worked. Take care, when winding completed areas of beadwork, to avoid distorting the lie of the beads.

To attach fabric to a frame:

1 Hem the edges of the fabric to strengthen them
2 Sew the top and bottom of the fabric to the top and bottom webbing
3 Assemble the frame and tighten the wing-nuts
4 Using a strong thread, lace the sides of the fabric to the stretchers and tighten so that the fabric is taut and ready to stitch.

BEADS

The beads used for the projects in this book are made of glass. They can be known as *rocailles*, meaning little stones or seeds, but are usually known as seed beads. They are uniformly round, making them ideal for embroidery. They are available in many sizes but for counted beadwork on 14-count Aida, size 11/0 is needed. Larger beads would not lie flat on this count of fabric. Loose beads that you have in your sewing basket may not necessarily be of the correct size.

Seed beads size 11/0 are available in a dazzling array of colours created by special finishes that are applied during manufacture. 'Silver' and 'gold' lined beads are lined with foil and reflect the light; iridescent beads are transparent with a delicate sheen; frosted beads are almost opaque; and lustre beads have a metallic sheen. Antique beads have an antique-look finish. By combining beads of different colours and finishes in one design you can achieve some stunning effects. The finishes are referred to by the abbreviations given in the list below.

For those of you who prefer to work on 18-count Aida, a range of size 14/0 beads is available. They are referred to in this book as miniature beads and are only available in a limited colour-range. You will need to use a beading needle to attach them to the fabric.

KEY TO BEAD FINISHES AND ABBREVIATIONS

(R)	Rainbow finish
(SLR)	Silver Lined Rainbow
(SL)	Silver Lined
(GL)	Gold Lined
(Ld)	Lined
(P)	Pearlised effect
(Matt)	Matt finish
(M)	Metallic
(I)	Iridescent
(C)	Clear
(Fr/F)	Frosted
(L)	Lustre
(A)	Antique
(CL)	Close, not exact, Mill Hill Conversion

All the designs in the book have been worked with Beadesign beads which are available in over two hundred dazzling colours and twelve finishes from needlework shops throughout the UK and by mail order. Throughout the book the Beadesign numbers and colours are given for each project. However, should you have difficulty in obtaining Beadesign beads, the corresponding colour-numbers of Mill Hill Beads have been given. (For suppliers, see page 119.) However, because the Mill Hill range of beads is smaller in number, precise conversions are not always available and many finished designs will not be exactly the same if Mill Hill beads are used. Readers should satisfy themselves that their chosen alternative colours are acceptable before embarking on a project.

Colour is very much a matter of personal preference and you may wish to personalise a design by choosing your own colour scheme. To enable you to do this a complete list of Beadesign beads is given on pages 115–18 along with Mill Hill equivalents.

Although Beadesign beads come in re-sealable bags of approximately 500, Mill Hill beads are sold in packets by weight – note that 100 beads weigh approximately 1g. Quantities of packets given for each project are for Beadesign beads.

BEAD CONTAINERS

Whilst working with beads, you will need a shallow container such as a tin lid or saucer for each colour. Line the containers with small pieces of felt to stop the beads from jumping around. This will make it much easier to pick them up on the needle. Any unused beads can be put back in their respective bags at the end of the project. Alternatively, you can buy commercially produced bead containers with individual compartments which enable you to store all your beads conveniently in the same place.

It is advisable to buy enough beads to complete your design at the outset as dye lots vary and exact colour-matches cannot be guaranteed. Do not expose beads to direct sunlight, as some colours may fade.

Readers who suffer from painful hands may find that by wearing Handeze Energising and Therapeutic Support Gloves they are able to sew for a considerable length of time without pain (see page 119).

N.B. FOR SAFETY REASONS, CHILDREN SHOULD NOT BE LEFT ALONE WITH BEADS OR A PIECE OF BEADWORK

STITCHES

The stitches used to attach the beads to the fabric are half cross stitches. You will also need to know how to sew back stitches and, for some designs in the book, how to form full cross stitches and French knots. Instructions and diagrams for forming all these stitches are given on pages 13–14. If you are unfamiliar with any stitch, it is wise to practise on an odd scrap of fabric before you begin work on a design.

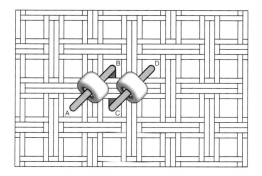

● *Applying beads using half cross stitch*

APPLYING BEADS

The beads are applied using half cross stitch. To start, use a tiny back stitch to secure the thread to the back of your work. Bring the needle up at A (see diagram), to the left of the row where the beads are to be sewn. Following the design chart, pick up the appropriate bead from your container with the point of your needle and allow it to slide down the thread to the fabric. Working over one block of Aida, insert your needle through the hole at B diagonally opposite and bring it up again through the hole directly below at C. Pick up the next bead and make the next stitch by inserting the needle at D. Where there are no symbols on the chart, no beads are worked. Leave one block of Aida without a bead for each of these squares. Work the design so that all the half cross stitches lie in the same direction. This is usually left to right but right to left is fine if you find it easier. Try to keep your stitch tension as even as possible and avoid attaching the beads too tightly. Do not leave a space of more than four beads without securing the thread on the wrong side of the fabric with a back stitch, to keep your beads taut and the tension even.

CROSS STITCH

When working full cross stitches with stranded cotton (embroidery floss) or flower thread, begin by inserting the needle from front to back, at A, three or four stitches to the right of your starting point, within the area to be worked (see diagram). Pull the thread through leaving a small tail on the front of the fabric. Return the needle to the front of the fabric by emerging at B, the bottom left-hand corner of the first stitch. Ensure that all the loose thread is pulled to the front but that the

end remains in place. Continue by making a complete row of half cross stitches, making sure that you cover the line of thread at the back of the work. When this is secure, snip off the tail close to the fabric.

At the end of the row, return to make a full cross using the same holes as before but working from right to left. The stitches should be next to each other, sharing the same holes and should all lie in the same direction. Do not jump from one area to another by carrying the thread across the back of the fabric. It will show through on the front when the work is mounted and will spoil the finished effect.

To finish off, run the thread through the back of the last few stitches taking care not to distort them. Make a tiny back stitch and snip off the thread.

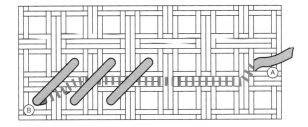

● *Starting to cross stitch (front of fabric)*

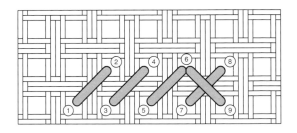

● *Completing a row of cross stitch*

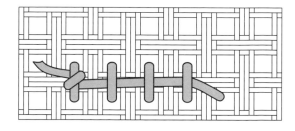

● *Finishing off (back of fabric)*

BACK STITCH

When applying beads, tiny back stitches are used to secure the thread to the back of the work both when you begin and when you finish off. They are also used for outlining some parts of designs where more definition is required, and for lettering and numbering. Back stitch is worked over one block of Aida either vertically, horizontally or diagonally. Begin by bringing the needle up at 1 (see diagram), down at 2, up at 3 and down at 1. Continue by coming up at 4 and down at 3, up at 5 and down at 4 and so on, following the line on the chart.

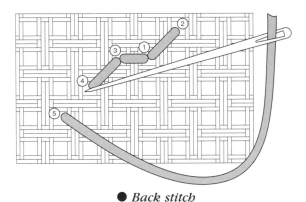

● *Back stitch*

FRENCH KNOTS

Using one strand of cotton (floss), bring the needle up to the front of the fabric at A (see diagram). Wind the thread round the needle once, or twice, depending on the size of the knot required. Hold the thread taut in the left hand (right, if you are left-handed), twist the needle back to A and insert it close to where the thread emerged. Hold the knot against the fabric, pull the thread through to the back and secure it with a tiny back stitch.

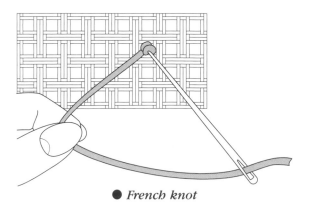

● *French knot*

CHOOSING A CHART

All charts in the book, whether for counted beadwork only, or for both beadwork and cross stitch, are based on the same principle; one square on the chart represents one block of Aida. Where there is a symbol in the squares of the chart, sew the appropriately coloured bead or cross. Every chart has a key to enable you to stitch the design as it appears in the photograph if you wish. Before beginning stitching it is always useful to match the symbols with the beads or threads they represent. This saves time and prevents mistakes later. Areas to be back stitched are also shown on the charts, where applicable, and are given in the key.

If you already have cross stitch charts without half or three-quarter stitches in the designs, you can work them completely, or partly, in beads. You may have to alter some colours to accommodate the range of beads available, but you are sure to produce a piece of work that is exciting and unique.

BEGINNING A PROJECT

You are now almost ready to put the first bead on to the fabric, but before you do there are a few final things to be done in preparation.

1 Wash your hands
2 Press the fabric to remove any creases
3 Fold the fabric into four to find the centre, open it out and mark the centre with a few tacking (basting) stitches along the folds. These can easily be removed when the work is complete
4 Oversew the edges of the fabric to prevent fraying
5 Place the fabric in a hoop if using one
6 Find the centre of the chart; this is clearly marked. Normally you should work from the centre outward. This ensures the design is correctly positioned and also helps to prevent the fabric from distorting
7 Having threaded your needle with a thread which matches the background material, stitch the central bead on to the fabric where the lines of tacking (basting) cross
8 At last your beadwork is underway. Relax and enjoy watching your design grow

Floral Alphabet

*T*HIS DELIGHTFUL ALPHABET *with its pretty border makes an impressive sampler. It can also be used to good effect for a variety of projects that are quick and easy to make. Individual initials, framed in an original way, make attractive gifts and the border around the alphabet can be used to make an unusual photograph frame.*

FLORAL ALPHABET SAMPLER

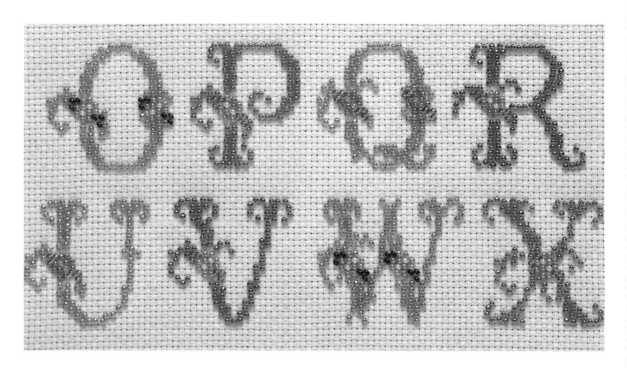

● *Detail of the floral alphabet sampler on page 16-17*

DESIGN SIZE 16¼ x 10½ inches (406 x 263mm)
STITCH COUNT 229 x 146

Zweigart white 14-count Aida 20 x 15 inches
   (500 x 375mm)
White polyester sewing thread
Sharps size 10 needle

BEADS

COLOUR	BEADESIGN	MILL HILL	BEADESIGN PACKETS
Mid blue	24	2006	Two
Dark emerald	42	332	One
Emerald	38	167	One
Jade	33	2008	Two
Medium lilac	17	2009	Four
Rainbow mauve	15	62047(F)	Five
Medium pink	5	2005	Three
Baby pink	4	145	One

1   It is advisable to use a frame to work this design (pages 9–10).

2   Find the centre of the fabric as described in Beginning a Project (page 14). It may be helpful to tack (baste) in with a contrasting thread every 10 or 20 squares to assist with counting.

3   Following the instructions in Applying Beads (page 13), begin stitching from the centre carefully following the chart on pages 18–19.

4   Work all the letters of the alphabet before stitching the border.

5   When the sampler is complete, check carefully to ensure that no beads have been missed. Wash and press your work following the instructions in Finishing and Mounting (pages 112–14).

6   The sampler was mounted in a textured wooden frame by a professional framer.

PHOTOGRAPH FRAME

DESIGN SIZE 7 x 8¾ inches (175 x 219mm)
STITCH COUNT 97 x 121

Charles Craft Aspen green 14-count Aida
    12 x 10 inches (300 x 250mm)
Green polyester sewing thread
Sharps size 10 needle
Craft Creations die-cut frame 7½ x 9½ inches
    (188 x 238mm) with 6¾ x 4¾ inches
    (169 x 119mm) oval aperture
Wadding (batting) to cover mount
Contrasting fabric to cover back of
    frame and stand

BEADS

COLOUR	BEADESIGN	MILL HILL	BEADESIGN PACKETS
Green/grey	112	332	Two
Clover pink	8	553	One

● *Floral alphabet sampler*

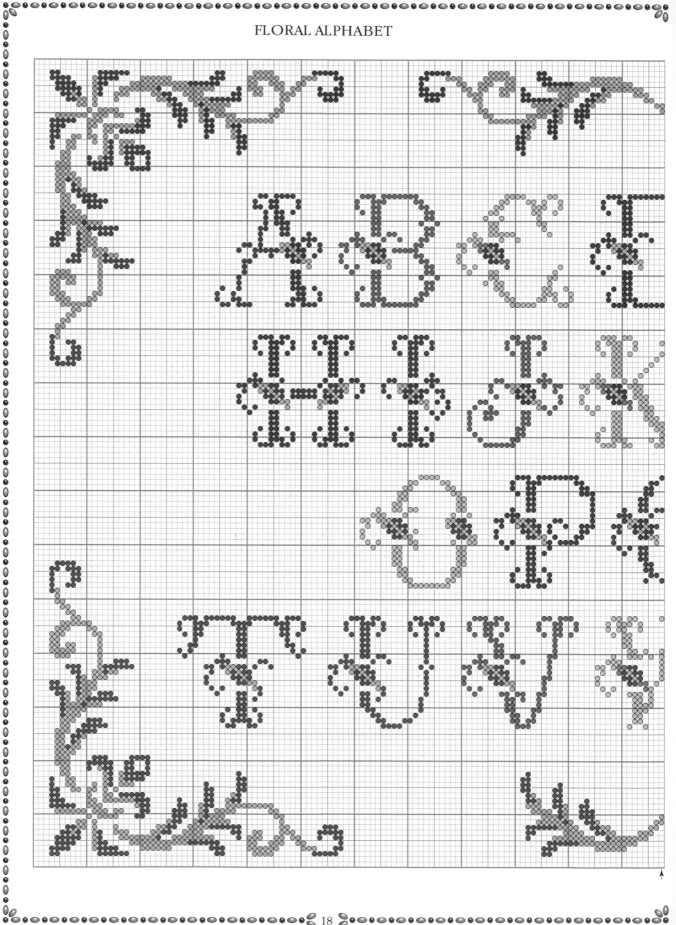

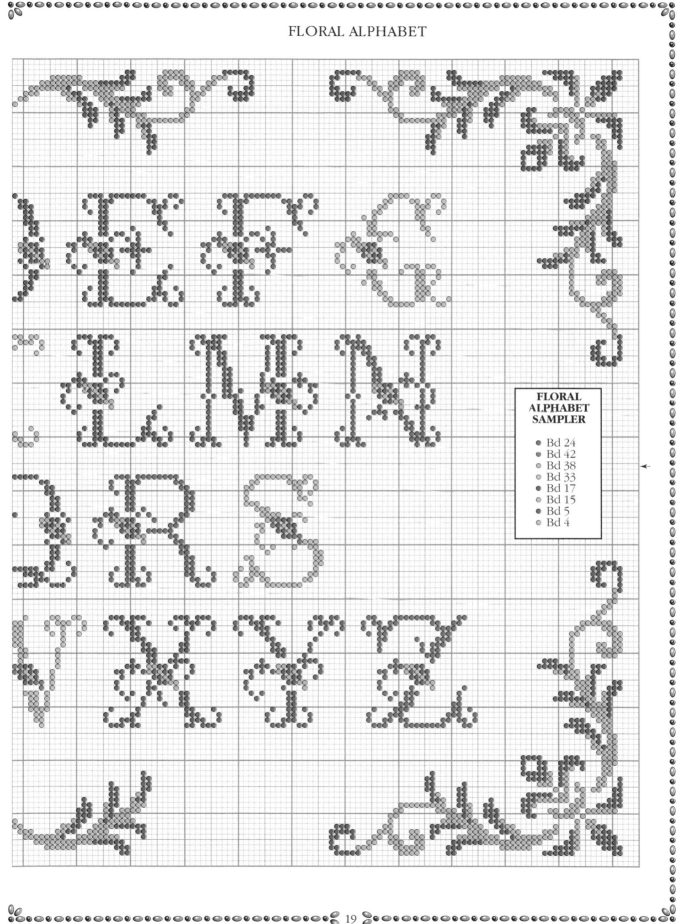

FLORAL ALPHABET SAMPLER

- Bd 24
- Bd 42
- Bd 38
- Bd 33
- Bd 17
- Bd 15
- Bd 5
- Bd 4

FLORAL ALPHABET

1 Begin by marking the position of the aperture and the finished size of the frame on the fabric with tacking (basting) stitches.

2 Position the border for the bottom right-hand corner of the frame as shown on the chart on the right.

3 The border for the top left-hand corner of the frame is taken from the same corner of the border surrounding the floral alphabet on pages 18–19. Using the section of chart given for this border, carefully position the corner for the photograph frame. Begin stitching from the top left-hand corner.

4 Make up the finished design by placing the wadding (batting) over the mount. Draw round the aperture and then carefully cut out the wadding (batting) from the area of the opening. Attach the wadding (batting) to the mount, using double-sided tape.

5 Position the work carefully over the wadding (batting).

6 Ensuring that the beadwork is level, fold the surplus fabric to the back of the mount and stick it down with double-sided tape. Cut a square of fabric from each corner to enable you to form a neat edge.

7 On the reverse side, cut a hole in the centre of the fabric. Snip carefully to within ¼ inch (6mm) of the edge of the aperture all the way round.

8 Apply adhesive to this remaining fabric, fold it to the inside of the aperture, and press it flat.

9 Cover the back of the frame and the stand with the contrasting fabric.

10 Position your photograph in the frame.

11 Alternatively, you could put the mount into a frame thus avoiding having to cover the back of it.

● *Photograph frame and individual initials*

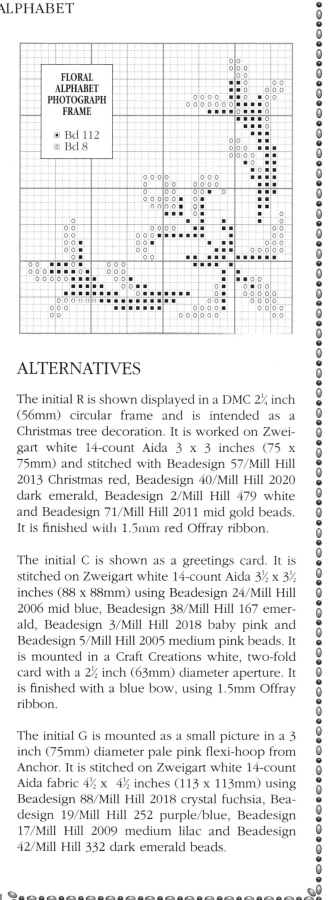

FLORAL
ALPHABET
PHOTOGRAPH
FRAME

■ Bd 112
◉ Bd 8

ALTERNATIVES

The initial R is shown displayed in a DMC 2¼ inch (56mm) circular frame and is intended as a Christmas tree decoration. It is worked on Zweigart white 14-count Aida 3 x 3 inches (75 x 75mm) and stitched with Beadesign 57/Mill Hill 2013 Christmas red, Beadesign 40/Mill Hill 2020 dark emerald, Beadesign 2/Mill Hill 479 white and Beadesign 71/Mill Hill 2011 mid gold beads. It is finished with 1.5mm red Offray ribbon.

The initial C is shown as a greetings card. It is stitched on Zweigart white 14-count Aida 3½ x 3½ inches (88 x 88mm) using Beadesign 24/Mill Hill 2006 mid blue, Beadesign 38/Mill Hill 167 emerald, Beadesign 3/Mill Hill 2018 baby pink and Beadesign 5/Mill Hill 2005 medium pink beads. It is mounted in a Craft Creations white, two-fold card with a 2½ inch (63mm) diameter aperture. It is finished with a blue bow, using 1.5mm Offray ribbon.

The initial G is mounted as a small picture in a 3 inch (75mm) diameter pale pink flexi-hoop from Anchor. It is stitched on Zweigart white 14-count Aida fabric 4½ x 4½ inches (113 x 113mm) using Beadesign 88/Mill Hill 2018 crystal fuchsia, Beadesign 19/Mill Hill 252 purple/blue, Beadesign 17/Mill Hill 2009 medium lilac and Beadesign 42/Mill Hill 332 dark emerald beads.

Nursery

THE ALPHABET shown here has been designed using lower-case letters and bright, cheerful colours to appeal to young children and to make a welcome addition to a child's bedroom. The Nursery Alphabet Sampler also includes several shapes, making the whole piece a useful teaching aid. Individual letters can also be used to personalise gifts or cards, or spell out a name as in the Name Plaques – ideal for children's bedrooms. Later in this section there is a Birth Sampler, with an original approach to welcoming a new baby.

NURSERY ALPHABET SAMPLER

DESIGN SIZE 12 x 11¾ inches (300 x 296mm)
STITCH COUNT 169 x 166

Zweigart white damask 14-count Aida
   17 x 17 inches (425 x 425mm)
White polyester sewing thread
Stranded cotton (embroidery floss) DMC 797/Madeira 912, DMC 701/Madeira 1305, DMC 666/Madeira 210, DMC 973/Madeira 105
Sharps size 10 needle
Tapestry size 24 needle

BEADS

COLOUR	BEADESIGN	MILL HILL	BEADESIGN PACKETS
Royal blue	27	0020	Two
Emerald green	37	62049(F)	Two
Deep yellow	48	128	Two
Christmas red	57	2013	Two

1 Find and mark the centre of your fabric as described in Beginning a Project (page 14). It is advisable to use a frame to work this design (see pages 9–10).

2 Using the tapestry needle and three strands of the embroidery thread (floss), work the rows of running stitches as shown on the chart. Once these rows are in place it will be easier to work the letters.

3 Using two strands of polyester sewing thread and the Sharps needle, attach the beads following the chart on pages 24–5.

4 When the work is complete, mount the sampler by lacing it on to mounting board (see page 114). The mounted sampler can then be inserted into a simple modern picture frame or used as a teaching aid.

N.B. FOR SAFETY REASONS, CHILDREN SHOULD NOT BE LEFT ALONE WITH BEADS OR A PIECE OF BEADWORK

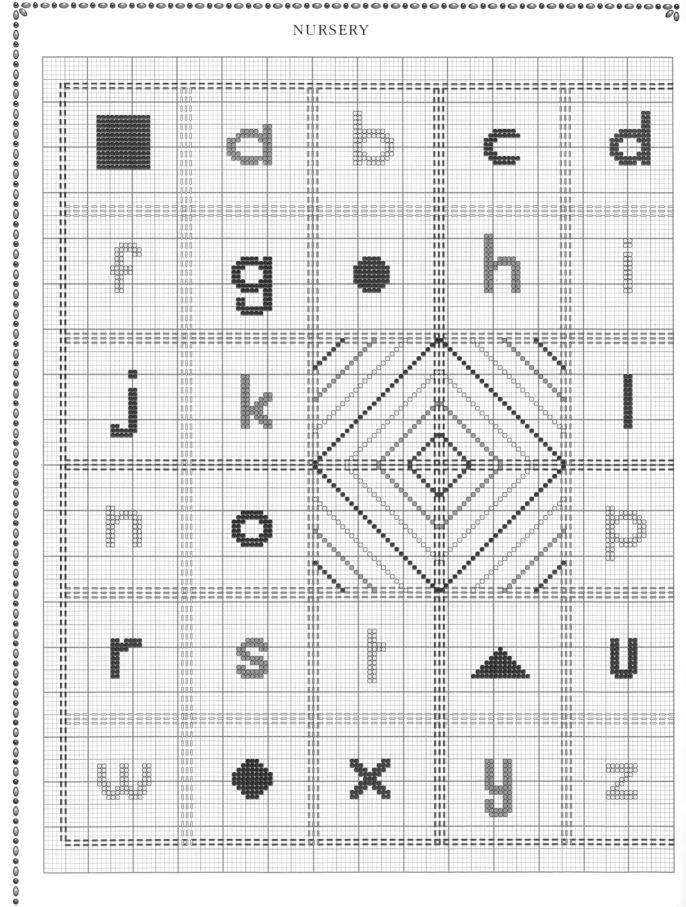

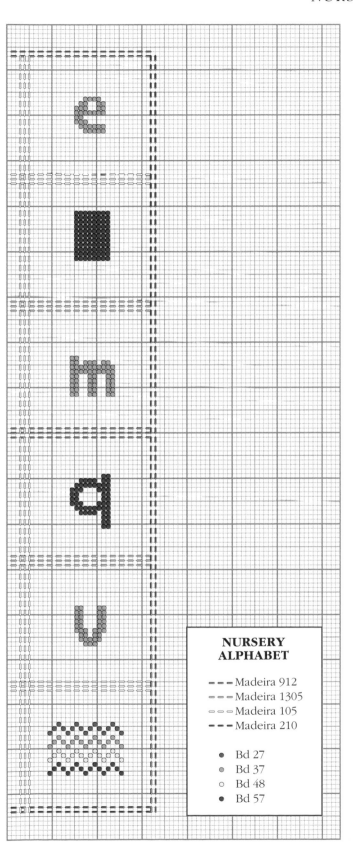

NURSERY ALPHABET

- - - Madeira 912
- - - Madeira 1305
- - - Madeira 105
- - - Madeira 210

- ● Bd 27
- ● Bd 37
- ○ Bd 48
- ● Bd 57

NAME PLAQUES

The letters of your child's name can be worked in any colour. You could select one favourite colour, or several to co-ordinate with the room – the possibilities are endless. To complete your name plaque, choose a border from the chart on pages 108–9, and you will have a very personal gift.

1 Using graph paper and the alphabet chart opposite, plot the name. Allow two squares between each letter to give sufficient space.

2 Choose and plot a border from the chart on pages 108–9 before you begin stitching the name, to ensure that you allow enough fabric for the complete design.

3 Stitch your design in your chosen colour-way. Try working the letters in pastel colours and adding an intricate border for a feminine effect.

4 Our models were mounted in standard 4 x 6 inch (100 x 150mm) photograph frames.

BIRTH SAMPLER

Welcome the arrival of a new baby by stitching this charming sampler. It was inspired by a phrase which Gillian's father used to describe her as a little girl: 'a twinkle in his eye'!

DESIGN SIZE 6 x 6 inches (150 x 150mm)
STITCH COUNT 84 x 82

Charles Craft navy 14-count Aida
  10 x 10 inches (250 x 250mm)
Navy polyester sewing thread
Stranded cotton (embroidery floss) DMC
762/Madeira 1804, DMC 318/Madeira 1802
Kreinik blending thread 001 HL
Kreinik cord 001C
Sharps size 10 needle
Tapestry size 24 needle

BEADS

COLOUR	BEADESIGN	MILL HILL	BEADESIGN PACKETS
Antique silver	68	3008	One
Deep black	65	3026	One
Mid grey	61	150	One
Star	C28		One

1 Find the centre of the material as described in Beginning a Project (page 14). Stitch the design following the chart below.

2 Work the stars at random in back stitch, using one strand of Kreinik cord in the tapestry needle.

3 Attach the star shape to the fabric at the point shown on the chart.

4 Stitch the window frame in cross stitch, following the chart and using two strands of stranded cotton (embroidery floss) and the tapestry needle.

5 Back stitch the lettering using two strands of stranded cotton (embroidery floss) combined with one strand of blending thread. Use the alphabet chart on page 31 to work the lettering.

6 This design was mounted in a professionally made frame. For instructions on mounting and framing, see pages 112–14.

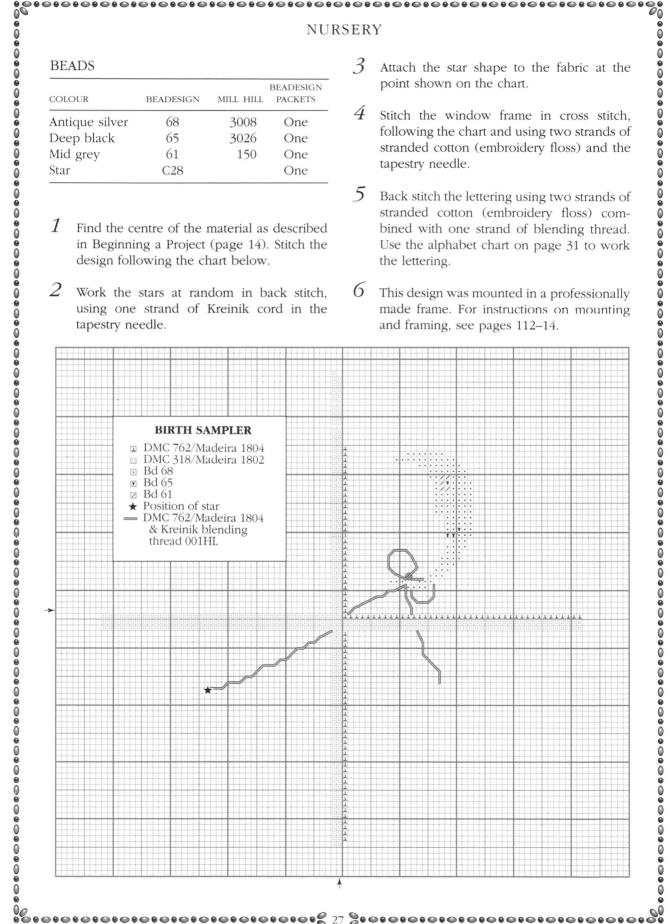

BIRTH SAMPLER

⊡ DMC 762/Madeira 1804
⊞ DMC 318/Madeira 1802
⊡ Bd 68
⊡ Bd 65
⊠ Bd 61
★ Position of star
— DMC 762/Madeira 1804
  & Kreinik blending
  thread 001HL

Weddings and Anniversaries

WEDDINGS AND ANNIVERSARIES *are perfect occasions to record with personalised samplers and cards. The designs shown are quick and easy to stitch and will make delightful gifts for newly married couples or for those celebrating many years of marriage.*

WEDDING SAMPLER

DESIGN SIZE 7½ x 6½ inches (187 x 163mm)
STITCH COUNT 105 x 90

Zweigart antique-white 14-count Aida
    11 x 10 inches (275 x 250mm)
White polyester sewing thread
Stranded cotton (embroidery floss) DMC 814/Madeira 514
Sharps size 10 needle
Tapestry size 24 needle

BEADS

COLOUR	BEADESIGN	MILL HILL	BEADESIGN PACKETS
Mid grey	62	283	One
Aqua	107	62043(F)	One
Dusty sapphire	106	2015	One
Deep amethyst	94	2025	One
Crystal fuchsia	88	2018	One
Amethyst iris heart	C10		Two

● *Wedding sampler*

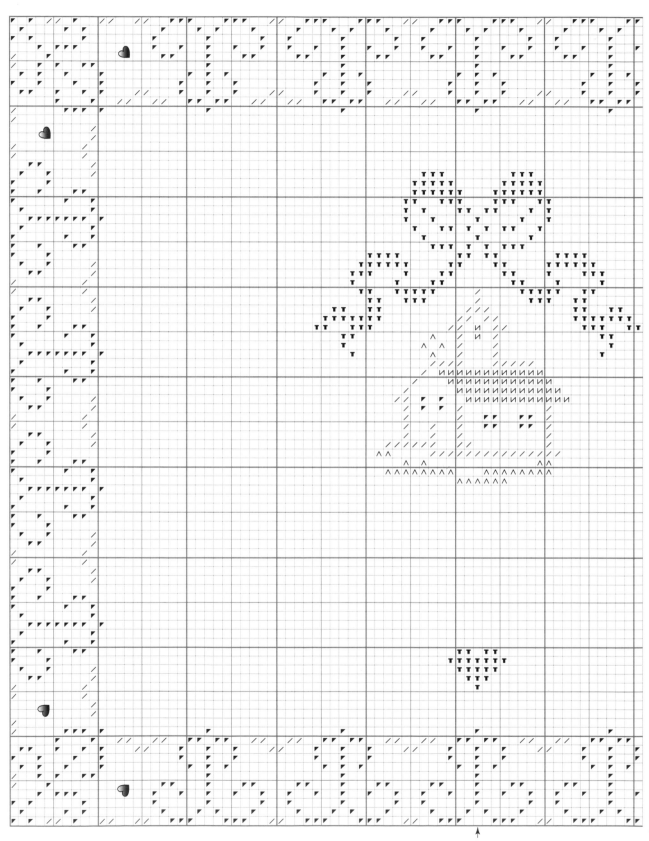

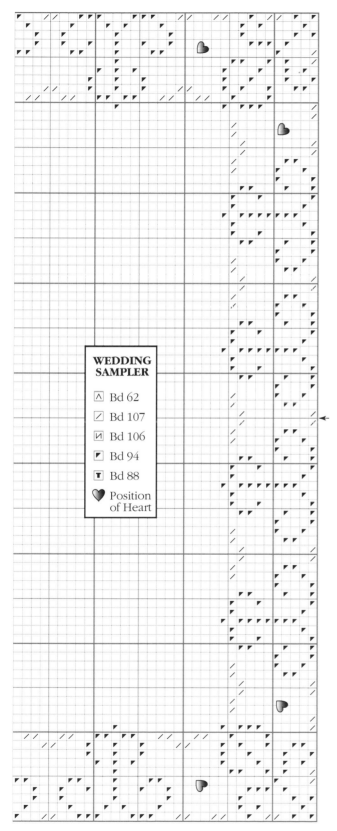

WEDDING SAMPLER

∧	Bd 62
⟋	Bd 107
⟍	Bd 106
◥	Bd 94
⊤	Bd 88
♥	Position of Heart

1 Find and mark the centre of your fabric as described in Beginning a Project (page 14). It is advisable to use a frame to work this design (see pages 9–10).

2 Chart the names and wedding date using the alphabet (above) and numbers shown on page 39. Stitch the sampler by following the chart on the left. Using the tapestry needle and two strands of cotton (floss), back stitch the names and date on to the sampler when the beadwork is complete.

3 The sampler on pages 28–9 was mounted in a professionally made frame.

HORSESHOE WEDDING CARD

Lucky horseshoes are traditional gifts for brides to receive. This card, with its delicate floral design, can be stitched in a variety of colourways to complement the bride's chosen colour scheme.

DESIGN SIZE 2½ x 3 inches (63 x 75mm)
STITCH COUNT 35 x 41

CORAL HORSESHOE COLOURWAY

Zweigart cream 14-count Aida
 5 x 5 inches (125 x 125mm)
Cream polyester sewing thread
DMC flower thread 2905
Sharps size 10 needle
Tapestry size 24 needle
Impress horseshoe-shaped card for mounting

BEADS

COLOUR	BEADESIGN	MILL HILL	BEADESIGN PACKETS
Light coral	54	275	One
Pearl	44	2001	One
Rose coral	49	2003	One
Emerald	38	167	One

BLUE HORSESHOE COLOURWAY

5 inch (125mm) square of light blue 14-count
 Aida
Light blue polyester sewing thread
Stranded cotton (embroidery floss) DMC
989/Madeira 1401

BEADS

COLOUR	BEADESIGN	MILL HILL	BEADESIGN PACKETS
Yellow	115	2019	One
Mid blue	23	168	One
Powder blue rainbow	147	2026	One
Light green	32	561	One

● *Horseshoe wedding cards shown in four different colourways*

PINK HORSESHOE COLOURWAY

5 inch (125mm) square of cream 14-count Aida
Cream polyester sewing thread
Stranded cotton (embroidery floss) DMC
989/Madeira 1401

BEADS

COLOUR	BEADESIGN	MILL HILL	BEADESIGN PACKETS
Bright silver	67	2010	One
Baby pink	4	145	One
Rose pink	6	2004	One
Emerald green	38	167	One

LILAC HORSESHOE COLOURWAY

5 inch (125mm) square of white 14-count Aida
White polyester sewing thread
Stranded cotton (embroidery floss) DMC
989/Madeira 1401

BEADS

COLOUR	BEADESIGN	MILL HILL	BEADESIGN PACKETS
Yellow	115	2019	One
Purple/blue	19	252	One
Medium lilac	17	2009	One
Emerald green	38	167	One

1 Find the centre of the design and the centre of the fabric as described on page 14.

2 Stitch the design in your chosen colourway following the chart below.

3 Back stitch the flower stems using the tapestry needle and flower thread or two strands of stranded cotton (embroidery floss).

4 For instructions on mounting into a card, refer to pages 112–13.

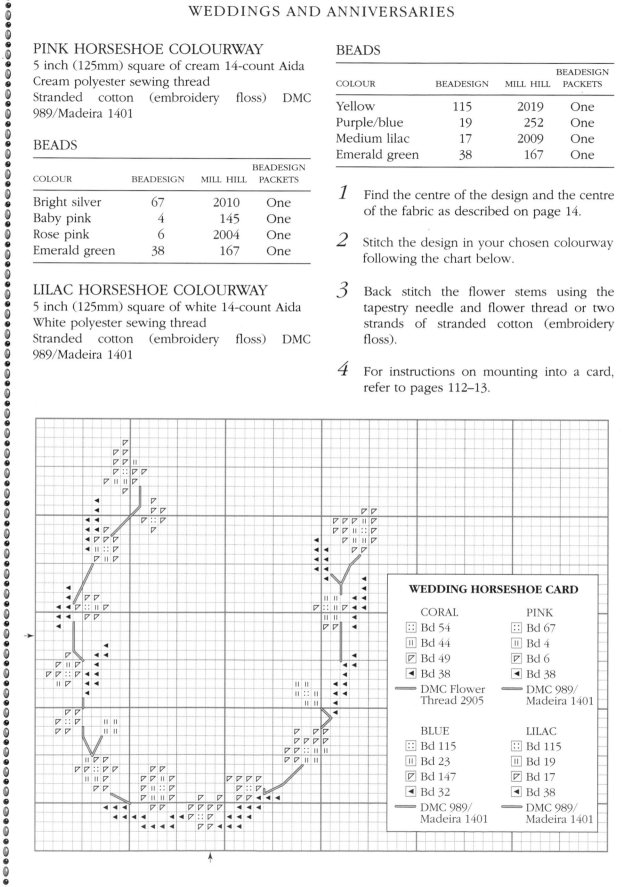

WEDDING HORSESHOE CARD

CORAL		PINK	
∷ Bd 54		∷ Bd 67	
‖ Bd 44		‖ Bd 4	
▽ Bd 49		▽ Bd 6	
◀ Bd 38		◀ Bd 38	
— DMC Flower Thread 2905		— DMC 989/ Madeira 1401	

BLUE		LILAC	
∷ Bd 115		∷ Bd 115	
‖ Bd 23		‖ Bd 19	
▽ Bd 147		▽ Bd 17	
◀ Bd 32		◀ Bd 38	
— DMC 989/ Madeira 1401		— DMC 989/ Madeira 1401	

WEDDING ANNIVERSARY CARDS OR PICTURES

This versatile design can be stitched in a choice of colourways and mounted either as a card or as a picture to commemorate a wedding anniversary. The design can also be used for a wedding card or picture by replacing the number at the top with the date of the wedding, using smaller numbers from page 39. You can also replace 'Congratulations' with the couple's names. Mount the design in a card or frame of your choice.

25th ANNIVERSARY

DESIGN SIZE 4 x 2¼ inches (100 x 56mm)
STITCH COUNT 58 x 32

Zweigart ivory 14-count Aida
  6 x 4 inches (150 x 100mm)
Ivory polyester sewing thread
Stranded cotton (embroidery floss) DMC
957/Madeira 0612
Sharps size 10 needle

Tapestry size 24 needle
25cm pink Offray ribbon, 1.5mm wide
Impress silver, medium oval, three-fold card for mounting

BEADS

COLOUR	BEADESIGN	MILL HILL	BEADESIGN PACKETS
Bright silver	67	2010	One
Medium pink	5	2005	One
Emerald	38	167	One

1 Begin by plotting 'congratulations' and numbers from the chart on page 39.

2 To stitch the card or picture, begin by finding the centre of the chart and the material. Mark the centre of the fabric following the instructions in Beginning a Project (page 14).

3 Stitch the design following the chart on page 38. Back stitch 'Congratulations' and numbers, using two strands of cotton (floss) in the tapestry needle.

4 Finish by threading the ribbon through the tapestry needle and sewing it through the fabric where indicated on the chart. Tie a bow and trim to the required length.

5 Instructions for mounting are given on pages 112–14.

40th ANNIVERSARY

DESIGN SIZE 4 x 2¼ inches (100 x 56mm)
STITCH COUNT 58 x 32

Zweigart cream 14-count Aida
  6 x 4 inches (150 x 100mm)
Cream polyester sewing thread
Stranded cotton (embroidery floss) DMC 814/Madeira 0514
Sharps size 10 needle
Tapestry size 24 needle
25cm wine Offray ribbon, 1.5mm wide
Craft Creations 4½ x 7 inches (112 x 175mm) round-corner oblong card with red, foil-printed borderline for mounting

BEADS

COLOUR	BEADESIGN	MILL HILL	BEADESIGN PACKETS
Plum	10	2012	One
Heather	14	206	One
Emerald	38	167	One

To stitch the card or picture, follow the instructions given for the 25th Wedding Anniversary Card on page 35.

50th ANNIVERSARY

DESIGN SIZE 4 x 2¼ inches (100 x 56mm)
STITCH COUNT 58 x 32

Zweigart cream 14-count Aida
  6 x 4 inches (150 x 100mm)

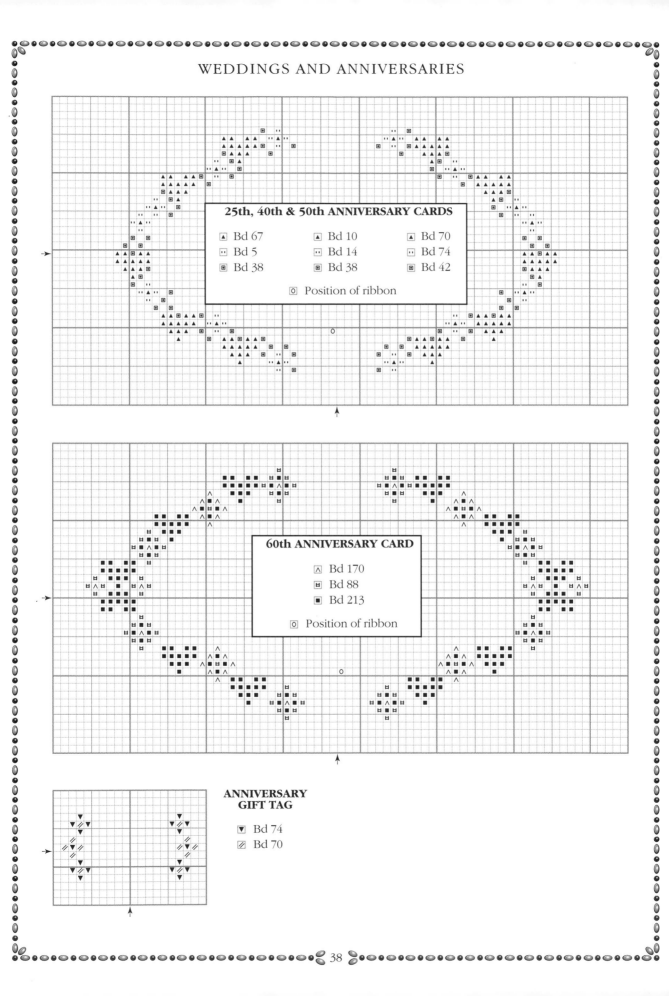

25th, 40th & 50th ANNIVERSARY CARDS

▲ Bd 67	▲ Bd 10	▲ Bd 70
∷ Bd 5	∷ Bd 14	∷ Bd 74
⊞ Bd 38	⊞ Bd 38	⊞ Bd 42

⊡ Position of ribbon

60th ANNIVERSARY CARD

∧	Bd 170
⊞	Bd 88
■	Bd 213

⊡ Position of ribbon

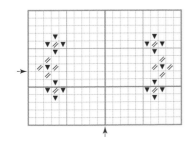

**ANNIVERSARY
GIFT TAG**

▼ Bd 74
⁄⁄ Bd 70

ABCDEFGHIJKLM
NOPQRSTUVWXYZ

abcdefghijklmnopqrstuvwxyz

1234567890

ABCDEFGHIJKLM
NOPQRSTUVWXYZ

abcdefghijklmnopqrstuvwxyz

ABCDEFGHIJKLM
NOPQRSTUVWXYZ

abcdefghijklm
nopqrstuvwxyz

1234567890 ?

Cream polyester sewing thread
Stranded cotton (embroidery floss) DMC 676/Madeira 2208
Sharps size 10 needle
Tapestry size 24 needle
25cm yellow-gold Offray ribbon, 1.5mm wide
Craft Creations 4½ x 7 inches (112 x 175mm) cut-corner oblong card with printed gold borderline for mounting

BEADS

COLOUR	BEADESIGN	MILL HILL	BEADESIGN PACKETS
Bright gold	70	2011	One
Copper	74	330	One
Dark emerald	42	332	One

1 To stitch the card or picture, follow the instructions given for the 25th Wedding Anniversary Card (pages 35–6).

2 The 50th Wedding Anniversary Picture was mounted in a dark wood, professionally made frame.

60th ANNIVERSARY

This design was stitched for Christine's grandparents' Diamond Wedding Anniversary, June 29th 1993. It is based on the 25th Wedding Anniversary Card on page 35, but includes diamonds to represent the number of years. The design was framed in a pale pink, professionally made frame and presented to the couple as a lasting reminder of this special occasion.

DESIGN SIZE 4¾ x 2¼ inches
STITCH COUNT 66 x 33

Zweigart antique-white 14-count Aida
   7 x 5 inches (175 x 125mm)
Off-white polyester sewing thread
DMC flower thread 2719
Sharps size 10 needle
Tapestry size 24 needle
25cm each, Offray ribbons – misty turquoise and colonial rose, 1.5mm wide
Impress silver, kingsize oval three-fold card for mounting

BEADS

COLOUR	BEADESIGN	MILL HILL	BEADESIGN PACKETS
Sky blue	170	2017	One
Crystal fuchsia	88	2018	One
Crystal pink	213	62048	One

To stitch the card or picture, follow the instructions given for the 25th Wedding Anniversary Card (pages 35–6).

ANNIVERSARY GIFT TAG

This small, quick and easy design can be adapted for any wedding anniversary by changing the colourway and number, using the numerals on page 39.

DESIGN SIZE 1¼ x ¾ inch (31 x 19mm)
STITCH COUNT 18 x 9

Zweigart cream 14-count Aida
   2 x 2 inches (50 x 50mm)
Cream polyester sewing thread
Stranded cotton (embroidery floss) DMC 676/Madeira 2208
Sharps size 10 needle
Tapestry size 24 needle
25cm yellow-gold Offray ribbon, 1.5mm wide
Impress 2 x 2¾ inches (50 x 69mm) silver, folding gift tag for mounting

BEADS

COLOUR	BEADESIGN	MILL HILL	BEADESIGN PACKETS
Copper	74	330	One
Bright gold	70	2011	One

1 Work from the centre of the material and the chart (see page 14), stitch the numerals in back stitch, using the tapestry needle and two strands of cotton (floss). When all the numerals have been stitched, apply the beads following the chart on page 38.

2 Details for mounting are given on pages 112–14.

3 Finish the gift tag with the ribbon.

Birthdays

*S*ɪɴᴄᴇ ᴠɪᴄᴛᴏʀɪᴀɴ ᴛɪᴍᴇꜱ, *the sending of greetings cards has been a popular way of showing our affection and regard for others. Although commercially produced cards for every occasion are widely available, it is always a pleasure to give or receive a hand-made card. The time and thought that has gone into its creation will mean a great deal to the recipient who can treasure it as a keepsake or frame it as a constant reminder of the occasion.*

RED AND PURPLE CARD

The design for the birthday cards shown on page 41 is simple and adaptable. Choose your own colour scheme and work your own greeting in back stitch. Use the alphabets on page 39 to choose a size of lettering that will allow you to stitch a longer name or greeting, or just add appropriate numbers.

The designs for the matching gift tags are taken from the main design and worked on stitching paper.

DESIGN SIZE 2¾ x 2 inches (69 x 50mm)
STITCH COUNT 27 x 30

Zweigart antique-white 14-count Aida
   4 x 4 inches (100 x 100mm)
Off-white polyester sewing thread
DMC flower thread 2732 for cross stitch
DMC flower thread 2394 for lettering
Sharps size 10 needle
Tapestry size 24 needle
Craft Creations birthday greetings card, blank, blue on cream with 3 inch (75mm) diameter aperture

BEADS

COLOUR	BEADESIGN	MILL HILL	BEADESIGN PACKETS
Mid yellow	80	2002	One
Deep red	120	165	One
Deep purple	185	62042(F)	One

1 Chart your chosen name or greeting from the alphabets on pages 31 and 39.

2 Find the centre of the design and the fabric, following the instructions on page 14, and work from this point outward, following the chart opposite.

3 The leaves of the design are worked in cross stitch, and the lettering in back stitch, using the tapestry needle and flower thread.

4 Refer to pages 112–14 for instructions on finishing and mounting.

MATCHING GIFT TAG

DESIGN SIZE 1 x ¾ inch (25 x 19mm)
STITCH COUNT 15 x 12

Jane Greenoff's stitching paper – white 4 x 3
   inches (100 x 75mm)
White polyester sewing thread
DMC flower thread 2732 for cross stitch
DMC flower thread 2394 for lettering
Sharps size 10 needle
Tapestry size 24 needle
25cm red Offray ribbon, 1.5mm wide

BEADS

COLOUR	BEADESIGN	MILL HILL	BEADESIGN PACKETS
Mid yellow	80	2002	One
Deep purple	185	62042(F)	One

1 Use two strands of polyester sewing thread for extra security when sewing on the beads.

2 Plot your greeting using the alphabet charts on pages 31 and 39 to ensure that it will fit.

3 Find the centre of the paper and then stitch the flower following the chart opposite. Back stitch your greeting.

4 Carefully cut your gift tag to the required size. Cut and stick another piece of stitching paper on to the back of the tag to hide the threads.

5 Finish with a ribbon bow.

BOWL WITH PINK AND MAUVE DESIGN

DESIGN SIZE 2¾ x 2 inches (69 x 50mm)
STITCH COUNT 37 x 30

Zweigart antique-white 14-count Aida
    4 x 4 inches (100 x 100mm)
Off-white polyester sewing thread
DMC flower thread 2937 for cross stitch
DMC flower thread 2333 for lettering
Sharps size 10 needle
Tapestry size 24 needle
Framecraft 2½ inch (63mm) diameter frosted-
    glass bowl for mounting

BEADS

COLOUR	BEADESIGN	MILL HILL	BEADESIGN PACKETS
Mustard yellow	176	62041	One
Pale purple	167	62034(F)	One
Fuchsia pink	177	62037(F)	One

1 Follow the stitching instructions given for the Red and Purple Card (page 42).

2 Refer to the manufacturer's instructions for mounting the design into the bowl.

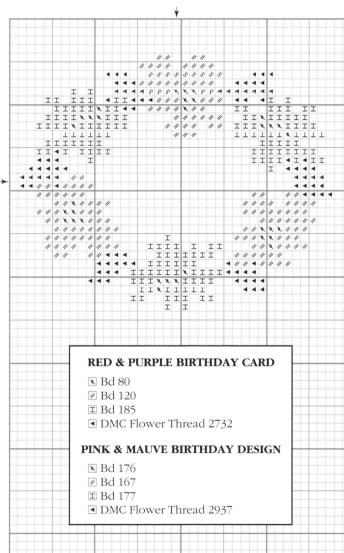

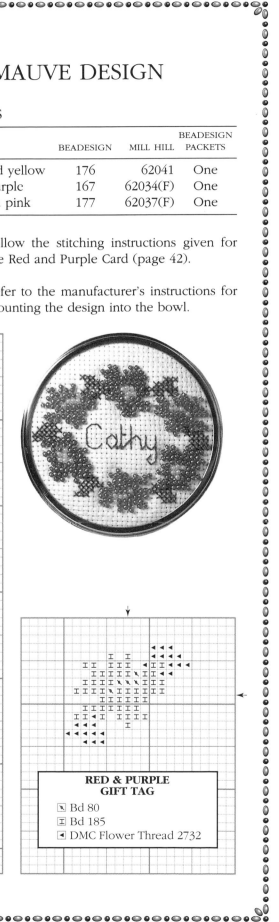

RED & PURPLE BIRTHDAY CARD

⬛ Bd 80
▨ Bd 120
I Bd 185
◀ DMC Flower Thread 2732

PINK & MAUVE BIRTHDAY DESIGN

⬛ Bd 176
▨ Bd 167
I Bd 177
◀ DMC Flower Thread 2937

RED & PURPLE GIFT TAG

⬛ Bd 80
I Bd 185
◀ DMC Flower Thread 2732

1   Find the centre of the material as described in Beginning a Project (page 14).

2   Stitch your chosen design following the chart on page 45. When stitching the Kite or Cockerel design, use two strands of cotton (floss) for the back stitch.

3   Instructions for mounting in cards are given on pages 112–13.

COCKEREL PICTURE

This little picture is worked on 18-count Aida using miniature beads which give a delicate finished result.

DESIGN SIZE 1 x 1 inch (25 x 25mm)
STITCH COUNT 18 x 18

Zweigart cream 18-count Aida 2 x 2 inches (50 x 50mm)
Cream polyester sewing thread
Stranded cotton (embroidery floss) DMC 797/Madeira 912
Beading needle
Tapestry size 24 needle
Mini pine frame 3½ inches (88mm) square, and yellow gift tag from Kraftie Kits.

BEADS

COLOUR	BEADESIGN	MILL HILL	BEADESIGN PACKETS
Deep yellow	4048	42011	One
Royal blue	4027	40020	One
Christmas red	4057	42013	One
Burnt orange	4052	42028	One
Emerald	4037	40332	One

1   Stitch the design following the instructions for the birthday cards (see above). Use one strand of cotton (floss) in the tapestry needle for back stitch.

2   Mount your work in the gift tag and then in the frame following the instructions given on pages 112–14.

18th and 21st BIRTHDAY CARDS

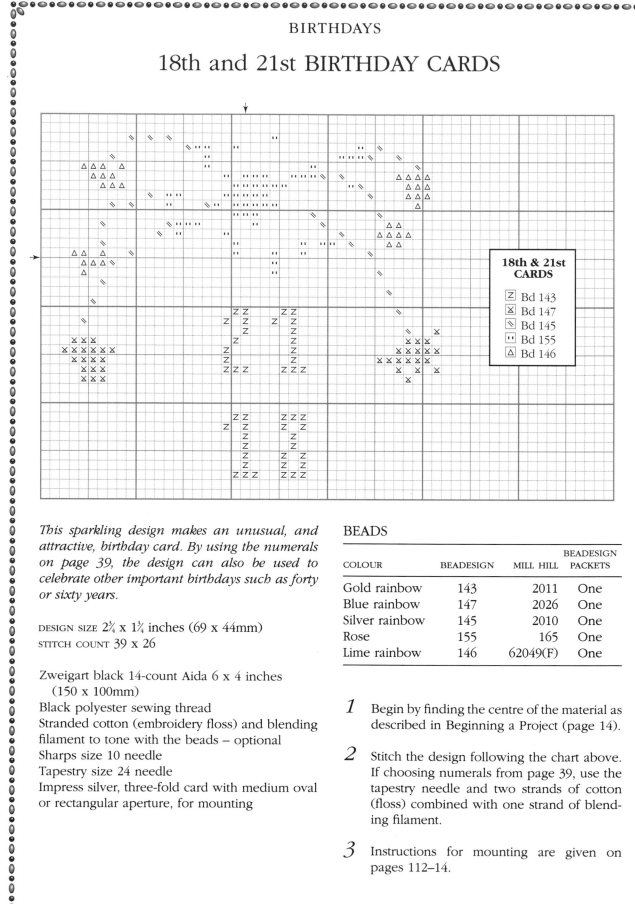

18th & 21st CARDS

Ƶ Bd 143
☒ Bd 147
⬉ Bd 145
'' Bd 155
△ Bd 146

This sparkling design makes an unusual, and attractive, birthday card. By using the numerals on page 39, the design can also be used to celebrate other important birthdays such as forty or sixty years.

DESIGN SIZE 2¾ x 1¾ inches (69 x 44mm)
STITCH COUNT 39 x 26

Zweigart black 14-count Aida 6 x 4 inches
(150 x 100mm)
Black polyester sewing thread
Stranded cotton (embroidery floss) and blending filament to tone with the beads – optional
Sharps size 10 needle
Tapestry size 24 needle
Impress silver, three-fold card with medium oval or rectangular aperture, for mounting

BEADS

COLOUR	BEADESIGN	MILL HILL	BEADESIGN PACKETS
Gold rainbow	143	2011	One
Blue rainbow	147	2026	One
Silver rainbow	145	2010	One
Rose	155	165	One
Lime rainbow	146	62049(F)	One

1 Begin by finding the centre of the material as described in Beginning a Project (page 14).

2 Stitch the design following the chart above. If choosing numerals from page 39, use the tapestry needle and two strands of cotton (floss) combined with one strand of blending filament.

3 Instructions for mounting are given on pages 112–14.

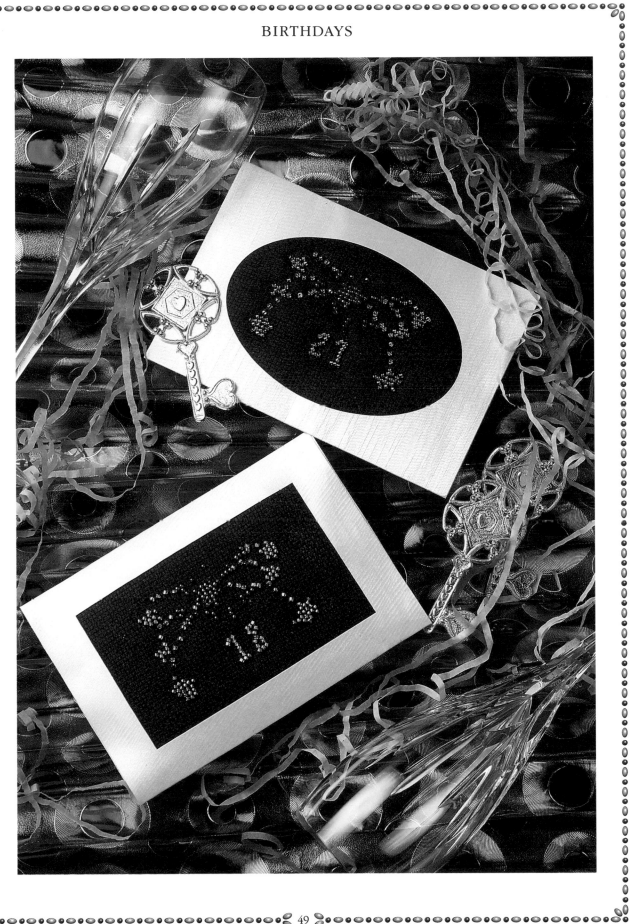

Summer
Flowers
and Fruit

❋ ❋

*T*HREE PRETTY DESIGNS *have been stitched and surrounded by a co-ordinating border to make a picture of summer flowers. Each design can also be used individually, with or without a border, and mounted in a variety of ways to make attractive gifts. You may wish to select your own colours for the flowers to make your work more personal.*

Continuing the summer theme, the Strawberry Tray introduces a design using our favourite fruit.

● *Summer flowers picture*

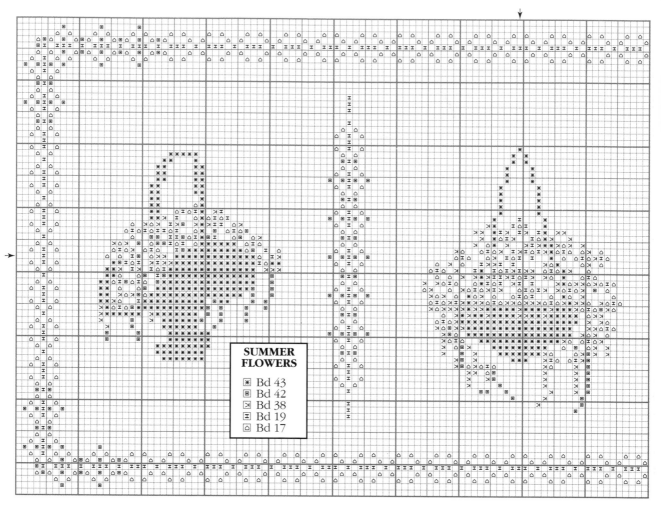

SUMMER FLOWERS

⊠ Bd 43
⊞ Bd 42
⊠ Bd 38
Ⅱ Bd 19
◁ Bd 17

SUMMER FLOWERS PICTURE

DESIGN SIZE 11¼ x 5¼ inches (287 x 131mm)
STITCH COUNT 157 x 73

Zweigart white 14-count Aida
  14½ x 8½ inches (363 x 213mm)
White polyester sewing thread
Sharps size 10 needle

BEADS

COLOUR	BEADESIGN	MILL HILL	BEADESIGN PACKETS
Antique green	43	2029	Two
Dark emerald	42	332	One
Emerald	38	167	One
Purple/blue	19	252	Two
Medium lilac	17	2009	Two

1 It is advisable to use a frame for working this design (see pages 9–10).

2 Find the centre of the fabric as described in Beginning a Project (page 14), and start stitching from the centre, following the chart above.

3 Stitch the three summer flower designs, and the vertical patterns that divide them, before stitching the border.

4 This picture was mounted in a professionally made frame with a double mount.

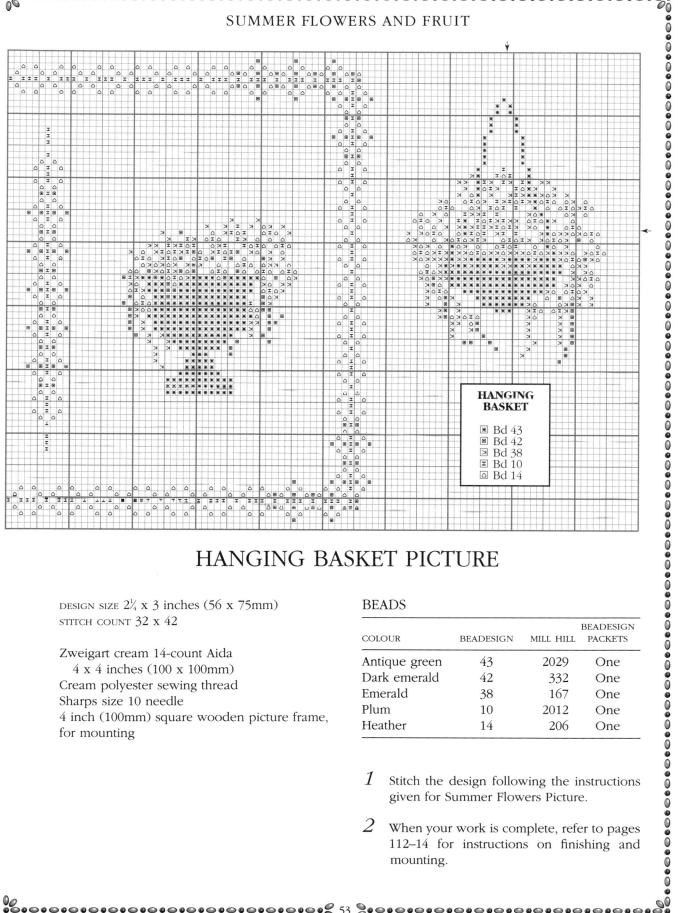

HANGING BASKET

✳	Bd 43
⊞	Bd 42
⊠	Bd 38
⅄	Bd 10
△	Bd 14

HANGING BASKET PICTURE

DESIGN SIZE 2¼ x 3 inches (56 x 75mm)
STITCH COUNT 32 x 42

Zweigart cream 14-count Aida
  4 x 4 inches (100 x 100mm)
Cream polyester sewing thread
Sharps size 10 needle
4 inch (100mm) square wooden picture frame,
for mounting

BEADS

COLOUR	BEADESIGN	MILL HILL	BEADESIGN PACKETS
Antique green	43	2029	One
Dark emerald	42	332	One
Emerald	38	167	One
Plum	10	2012	One
Heather	14	206	One

1 Stitch the design following the instructions given for Summer Flowers Picture.

2 When your work is complete, refer to pages 112–14 for instructions on finishing and mounting.

● *Hanging basket*

STRAWBERRY TRAY

This delightful strawberry tray reminds us of long summer days when we take leisurely teas in the garden. It is stitched in myriad lush colours, to reflect the qualities of both the plant and the season. The design would look equally attractive framed as a picture for your kitchen wall.

DESIGN SIZE 3¾ x 4¾ inches (94 x 119mm)
STITCH COUNT 53 x 66

Zweigart eau-de-nil 14-count Aida
  12 x 12 inches (300 x 300mm)
Eau-de-nil polyester sewing thread
DMC flower thread 2782
DMC flower threaad 2986
Sharps size 10 needle
Tapestry size 24 needle
Framecraft small tray 9½ inches (238mm) square –
'The Sudbery Collection' – for mounting

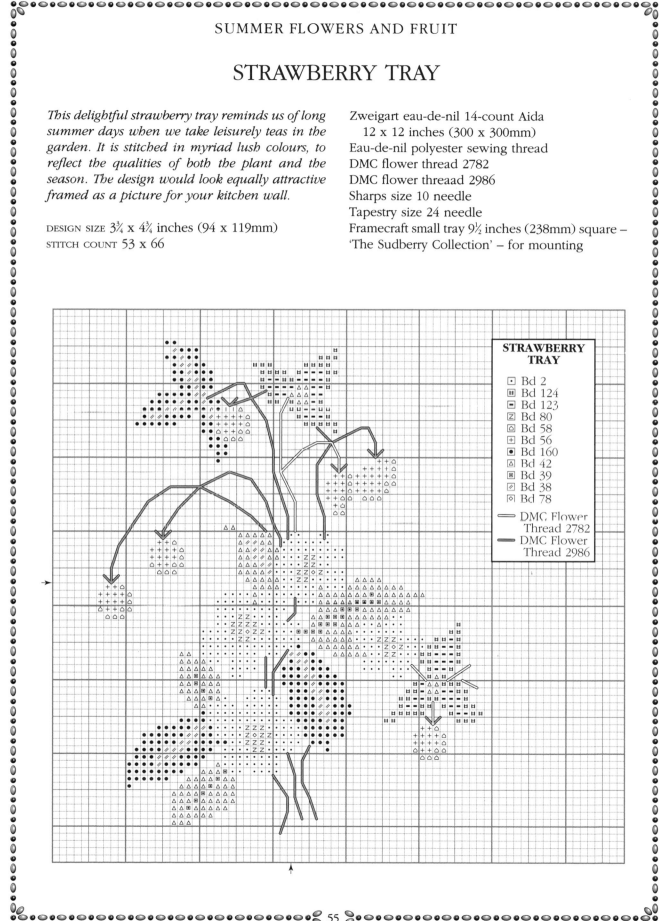

STRAWBERRY TRAY

⊡ Bd 2
⊞ Bd 124
⊟ Bd 123
☑ Bd 80
⬠ Bd 58
⊞ Bd 56
⊡ Bd 160
△ Bd 42
⊞ Bd 39
⬲ Bd 38
◉ Bd 78

━ DMC Flower
    Thread 2782
━ DMC Flower
    Thread 2986

BEADS

COLOUR	BEADESIGN	MILL HILL	BEADESIGN PACKETS
White	2	479	One
Gold	124	3036	One
Honey	123	2019	One
Mid yellow	80	2002	One
Christmas red	58	968	One
Christmas red	56	2013	One
Darkest green	160	2020	One
Dark emerald	42	332	One
Emerald	39	431	One
Emerald	38	167	One
Black	78	2014	One

1 Find the centre of the fabric as described in Beginning a Project (page 14), and start stitching from the centre, following the chart on page 55.

2 It is advisable to use a frame for working this design.

3 The stems of the leaves and fruits are worked in back stitch using the flower thread and tapestry needle.

4 Mount your finished work in the tray, following the manufacturer's instructions.

● *Strawberry tray*

Bees and Clover

*T*HE HUMMING OF BEES, *synonymous with summer, always conjures up an image of warm, lazy days. This delightful picture (with matching gift tag) would be a perfect gift for a summer birthday.*

BEE AND CLOVER PICTURE

DESIGN SIZE 3¼ x 3 inches (81 x 75mm)
STITCH COUNT 46 x 42

Zweigart antique-white 14-count Aida
   8 x 8 inches (200 x 200mm)
Off-white polyester sewing thread
DMC flower thread 2905 for back stitch
DMC flower thread 2937 for cross stitch
Kreinik metallic thread 060
Sharps size 10 needle
Tapestry size 24 needle

BEADS

COLOUR	BEADESIGN	MILL HILL	BEADESIGN PACKETS
Deep black	65	3026	One
Yellow	115	2019	One
Dark emerald	42	332	One
Emerald matt	39	431	One
Clover pink	96	2024	One
Light ruby	93	2024	One
Fuchsia pink	177	62037(F)	One

1 Find the centre of the fabric as described in Beginning a Project (page 14) and start stitching from the centre, following the chart on page 60.

2 Using the appropriate colour of flower thread and the tapestry needle, add the cross stitch and back stitch.

3 Back stitch the bee's wings and legs, using two strands of Kreinik thread in the tapestry needle.

4 Add the French knots to the wings, as indicated in the chart, using two strands of Kreinik thread.

5 Back stitch the veins of the wings, using one strand of Kreinik thread.

6 This picture was professionally mounted in a pale green wooden frame with a circular mount.

BEE GIFT TAG

This pretty gift tag is sewn on stitching paper. Use the Bee and Clover chart on page 60 to stitch the bee and then, using the alphabet charts on page 39, plot and stitch your own greeting or the recipient's name.

DESIGN SIZE 3¼ x 1¼ inches (81 x 31mm)
STITCH COUNT 46 x 19

Jane Greenoff's stitching paper – white
   4 x 3 inches (100 x 75mm)
White polyester sewing thread
DMC flower thread 2726 for lettering
DMC flower thread 2310 for bee's wings and legs
Kreinik metallic thread 060
Sharps size 10 needle
Tapestry size 24 needle
25cm bright yellow Offray ribbon, 1.5mm wide

● *Bee and clover picture*

BEES AND CLOVER

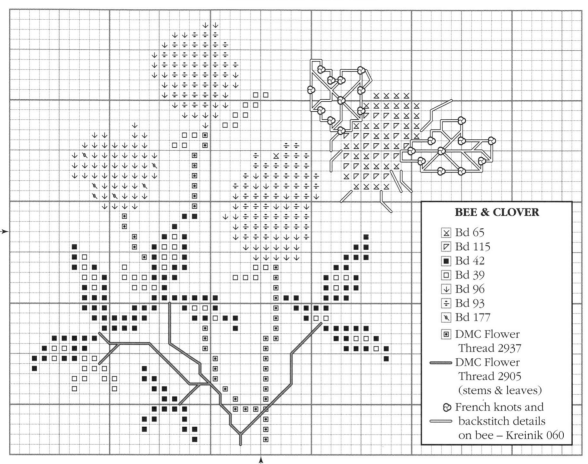

BEE & CLOVER

☒	Bd 65
⊡	Bd 115
■	Bd 42
☐	Bd 39
↓	Bd 96
÷	Bd 93
◱	Bd 177
⊡	DMC Flower Thread 2937
—	DMC Flower Thread 2905 (stems & leaves)
✿	French knots and
—	backstitch details on bee – Kreinik 060

BEADS

COLOUR	BEADESIGN	MILL HILL	BEADESIGN PACKETS
Deep black	65	3026	One
Yellow	115	2019	One

1   Plot your greeting, using the alphabet charts on page 39, to ensure that it will fit.

2   Find the centre of the paper and stitch the bee by following the Bee and Clover chart (above), but using two strands of sewing thread for extra security.

3   Combine one strand of metallic thread with the flower thread and back stitch the bee's wings and legs, using the tapestry needle.

4   Use two strands of metallic thread for the veins and French knots on the wings.

5   Combine one strand of metallic thread with the flower thread, and back stitch your greeting.

6   Carefully cut your gift tag to the required size. Cut and stick another piece of stitching paper on to the back of the tag to hide the threads.

7   Finish with a ribbon bow.

Butterflies

THE COLLAGE OF BUTTERFLIES *on pages 62–3 is intended as a design library for readers to use as they wish. The butterflies can be used in many different ways: for cards, gifts, or as part of a larger design such as a sampler. It is difficult to create totally accurate beadwork butterflies because of the vast number of shades needed.*

BUTTERFLY SAMPLER

DESIGN SIZE 8¼ x 7¼ inches (206 x 181mm)
STITCH COUNT 117 x 100

Zweigart cream 14-count Aida
  15 x 12 inches (375 x 300mm)
Cream polyester sewing thread
Stranded cottons (embroidery floss), or blending filaments, for the bodies and antennae, in colours to tone with each butterfly
Sharps size 10 needle
Tapestry size 24 needle

The extensive range of beads used for this sampler is listed on page 62.

1 It is advisable to work this design in a frame (see pages 9–10).

2 Begin by finding the centre of the material as described in Beginning a Project (page 14).

3 Stitch the design from the centre outward, following the chart on pages 62–3. It is advisable to complete all the beadwork before adding the bodies in cross stitch and the antennae in back stitch.

4 Mount and frame the work as required, following the instructions on pages 112–14.

BUTTERFLY CARD

DESIGN SIZE 2¼ x 1¾ inches (56 x 44mm)
STITCH COUNT 33 x 25

Charles Craft pale blue 14-count Aida
  6 x 4 inches (150 x 100mm)
Pale blue polyester sewing thread
Kreinik gold blending thread
Sharps size 10 needle
Tapestry size 24 needle
Craft Creations 3¼ inch (81mm) square, bright blue card with heart-shaped aperture

BEADS

COLOUR	BEADESIGN	MILL HILL	BEADESIGN PACKETS
French navy	194	60268(F)	One
Medium sapphire	172	168	One
Blue/purple	102	252	One
Purple/blue	19	252	One

1 Find the centre of the material (see page 14), and stitch the design following the chart for the deep blue butterfly on the sampler (pages 62–3).

2 Back stitch the antennae, using two strands of Kreinik thread in the tapestry needle. The body is worked in cross stitch using two strands of Kreinik thread.

3 Mount the card following the instructions on pages 112–13.

BEADS

COLOUR	BEADESIGN	MILL HILL	BEADESIGN PACKETS
Mid grey	61	150	One
Copper	74	330	One
Topaz	197	62057(F)	One
Olive	122	62057(F)	One
Honey	123	2019	One
Cream	152	123	One
Deep yellow	48	128	One
Deep yellow	117	62041(F)	One
Mid blue	24	2006	One
Mid blue	23	168	One
Baby blue	22	146	One
Light blue	20	2017	One
French navy	194	60168(F)	One
Turquoise	108	143	One
Turquoise	109	62038(F)	One
Light blue	21	143	One
Medium sapphire	172	168	One
Sky blue	174	2007	One
Ruby/gold	131	3033	One
Plum	10	2012	One
Medium pink	5	2005	One
Rainbow pink	3	2018	One
Burnt orange	52	423	One
Rose pink	6	2004	One
Rose coral	49	2003	One
Soft peach	158	150	One
Sea green	138	2015	One
Jade	33	2008	One
Palest green	110	161	One
Sea spray	190	2016	One
Pale blue	193	62046	One
Hint of green	168	2016	One
Medium lilac	17	2009	One
Blue/purple	102	252	One
Pale yellow	47	62039(F)	One
Daffodil	140	62041(F)	One
Mid yellow	80	2002	One
Deep lilac	164	62042(F)	One
Lilac	163	3023	One
Purple/blue	19	252	One
Rainbow mauve	15	62047(F)	One
Purple	99	283	One
Deep dusty pink	91	3019	One
Heather	14	206	One
Baby pink	4	145	One

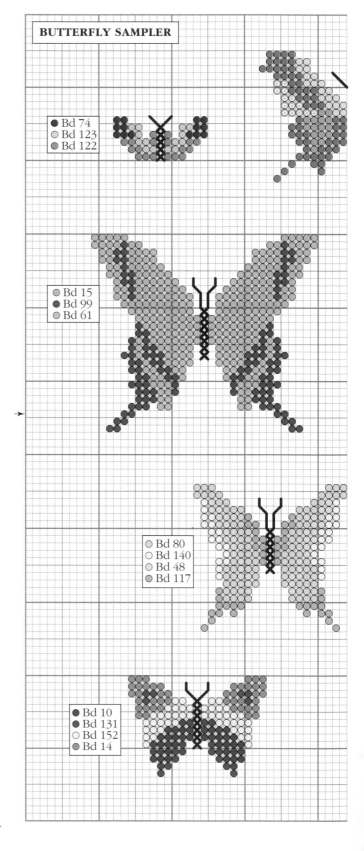

BUTTERFLY SAMPLER

Bd 74
Bd 123
Bd 122

Bd 15
Bd 99
Bd 61

Bd 80
Bd 140
Bd 48
Bd 117

Bd 10
Bd 131
Bd 152
Bd 14

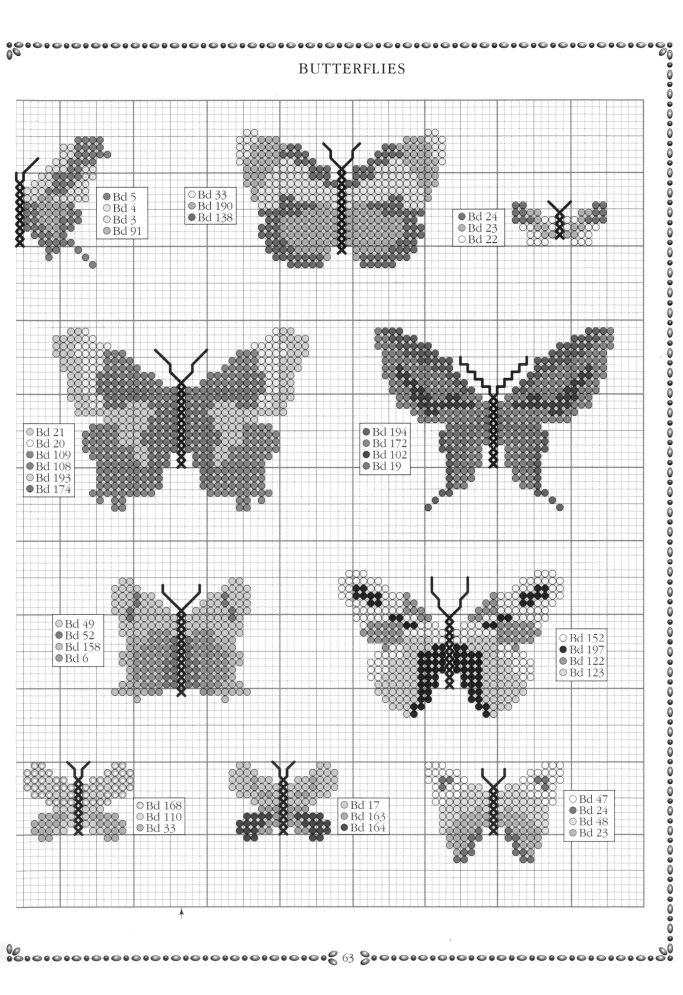

● Bd 5
○ Bd 4
○ Bd 3
● Bd 91

○ Bd 33
● Bd 190
● Bd 138

● Bd 24
● Bd 23
○ Bd 22

● Bd 21
○ Bd 20
● Bd 109
● Bd 108
○ Bd 193
● Bd 174

● Bd 194
● Bd 172
● Bd 102
● Bd 19

○ Bd 49
● Bd 52
● Bd 158
● Bd 6

○ Bd 152
● Bd 197
● Bd 122
○ Bd 123

● Bd 168
○ Bd 110
● Bd 33

● Bd 17
● Bd 163
● Bd 164

○ Bd 47
● Bd 24
○ Bd 48
● Bd 23

BUTTERFLY BOX LID

DESIGN SIZE 2¼ x 1½ inches (56 x 38mm)
STITCH COUNT 31 x 20

Jane Greenoff's cream stitching paper
   4 x 3 inches (100 x 75mm)
Cream polyester sewing thread
An oddment of dark brown stranded cotton
(embroidery floss)
Sharps size 10 needle
Tapestry size 24 needle
Framecraft 2⅞ x 2 inches (72 x 50mm), ivory, oval
box for mounting

BEADS

COLOUR	BEADESIGN	MILL HILL	BEADESIGN PACKETS
Topaz	197	62057(F)	One
Olive	122	62057(F)	One
Honey	123	2019	One
Cream	152	123	One

1   Find the centre of the stitching paper (see page 14), and work the design following the chart for the brown and cream butterfly, using two strands of sewing thread for extra security.

2   Back stitch the antennae using two strands of stranded cotton (embroidery floss) in the tapestry needle. The body is worked in cross stitch using two strands of stranded cotton (embroidery floss).

3   Mount according to the manufacturer's instructions, but do not cover the beads with the acetate disc as it may distort them.

● *A butterfly sampler, card and box lid show how versatile the butterfly design can be*

Hallowe'en

STITCH THESE THREE *spooky designs to bring a little magic into your Hallowe'en celebrations. All three designs have been worked in a flexi-hoop, combining different threads and bead-work. A metallic thread has been incorporated to give a sparkle to each design.*

GHOST

DESIGN SIZE 2½ x 2¾ inches (64 x 69mm)
STITCH COUNT 35 x 37

Charles Craft navy 14-count Aida
   6 x 6 inches (150 x 150mm)
Navy polyester sewing thread
Stranded cotton (embroidery floss) DMC 900/Madeira 0208, DMC 946/Madeira 0207, DMC 721/Madeira 0308
Kreinik blending thread 021
Sharps size 10 needle
Tapestry size 24 needle
25cm torrid orange Offray ribbon, 1.5mm wide
Anchor 4in (100mm), navy flexi-hoop

BEADS

COLOUR	BEADESIGN	MILL HILL	BEADESIGN PACKETS
Mid grey	61	150	One
White	2	479	One
Black	66	0081	One

● *Spooky hallowe'en ghost, bat and monster*

THE GHOST
- ⊠ Bd 61
- ⊞ Bd 2
- ⊙ Bd 66
- ⬆ DMC 900
  (or Madeira 0208)
  & Kreinik 021
- ⊙ DMC 946
  (or Madeira 0207)
  & Kreinik 021
- ⊞ DMC 721
  (or Madeira 0308)
  & Kreinik 021

THE BAT
- ◩ Bd 52
- ⬕ Bd 50
- ⦿ Bd 66
- — DMC Silver
  metallic thread

THE MONSTER
- ▼ Bd 57
- ⊡ Bd 38
- Ⓗ Bd 146
- — DMC Silver
  metallic thread

1. The flexi-hoop can be used as a frame for working this design.

2. Find the centre of the fabric as described in Beginning a Project (page 14).

3. Stitch the design following the chart on page 66.

4. 'Boo' is worked in cross stitch using the tapestry needle and two strands of stranded cotton (embroidery floss) combined with one strand of Kreinik thread.

5. Instructions for mounting into a flexi-hoop are given on page 113.

6. Finish by tying the ribbon through the loop at the top of the flexi-hoop.

MONSTER

DESIGN SIZE 1¼ x 2 inches (31 x 50mm)
STITCH COUNT 19 x 27

Charles Craft navy 14-count Aida
   4½ x 4½ inches (113 x 113mm)
Navy polyester sewing thread
DMC silver metallic thread
Sharps size 10 needle
Tapestry size 24 needle
25cm apple green Offray ribbon, 1.5mm wide
Anchor 3 inch (75mm), navy flexi-hoop

BEADS

COLOUR	BEADESIGN	MILL HILL	BEADESIGN PACKETS
Christmas red	57	2013	One
Emerald	38	167	One
Lime rainbow	146	62049(F)	One

1. Stitch the design following the instructions for the Ghost (above).

2. The teeth and antennae are worked in back stitch using one strand of silver thread in the tapestry needle.

BAT

DESIGN SIZE 2¾ x 3 inches (68 x 75mm)
STITCH COUNT 37 x 41

Charles Craft navy 14-count Aida
   6 x 6 inches (150 x 150mm)
Navy polyester sewing thread
DMC silver metallic thread
Sharps size 10 needle
Tapestry size 24 needle
25cm Indian orange Offray ribbon, 1.5mm wide
Anchor 4 inch (100mm), navy flexi-hoop

BEADS

COLOUR	BEADESIGN	MILL HILL	BEADESIGN PACKETS
Burnt orange	52	423	One
Tangerine	50	423	One
Black	66	0081	One

1. Stitch the design following the instructions for the Ghost.

2. The spider and the web are worked in two strands of metallic thread in back stitch and cross stitch, using the tapestry needle.

Valentine

*S*URPRISE YOUR VALENTINE *with a romantic gift (page 72) or with this pretty card and matching gift tag. Choose appropriate initials from the alphabets on page 39, or, to add a little mystery to this traditional Saint's day, substitute a question mark for the initials.*

VALENTINE

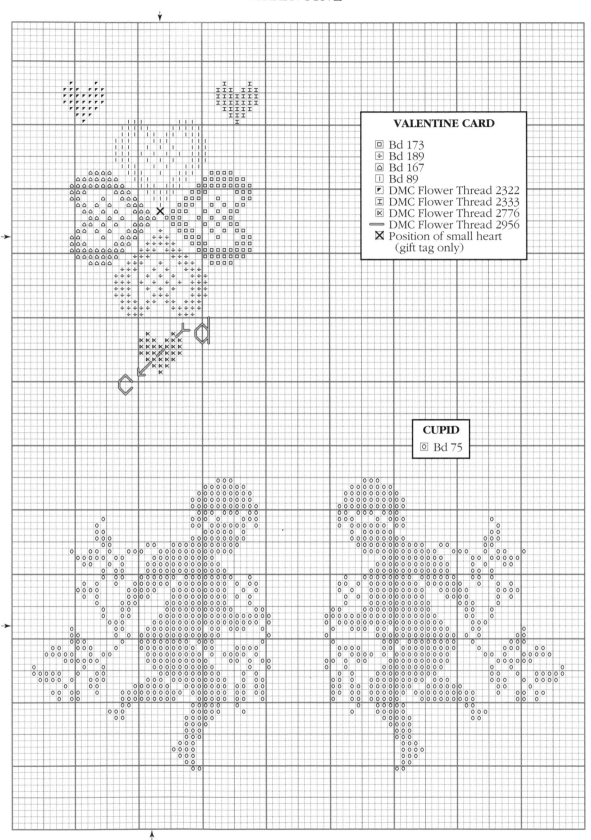

VALENTINE CARD

- ▣ Bd 173
- ⊞ Bd 189
- ⬠ Bd 167
- Ⅰ Bd 89
- ◨ DMC Flower Thread 2322
- Ⅰ DMC Flower Thread 2333
- ⊠ DMC Flower Thread 2776
- — DMC Flower Thread 2956
- ✗ Position of small heart
  (gift tag only)

CUPID

- ▣ Bd 75

VALENTINE CARD

DESIGN SIZE 2¼ x 3½ inches (56 x 88mm)
STITCH COUNT 31 x 49

Zweigart white 14-count Aida
  3 x 4 inches (75 x 100mm)
White polyester sewing thread
DMC flower thread 2322, 2333, 2776 for cross stitch
DMC flower thread 2956 for back stitch
Sharps size 10 needle
Tapestry size 24 needle
Impress silver, heart-shaped card for mounting

BEADS

COLOUR	BEADESIGN	MILL HILL	BEADESIGN PACKETS
Sapphire blue	173	2006	One
Sea jade	189	62038(F)	One
Pale purple	167	62034(F)	One
Hot pink	89	62035(F)	One

1 Find the centre of the material as described in Beginning a Project (page 14).

2 Work the design following the chart opposite. The four central hearts are worked in beads. The three small hearts are worked in cross stitch and the arrow and initials, or question mark, are worked in back stitch using the flower thread and tapestry needle. Complete the beadwork first.

3 When the stitching is complete, mount the design in the card, following the instructions given on pages 112–13.

VALENTINE GIFT TAG

This simple design is taken from the Valentine card and could be worked in any of the four colourways used for the card.

DESIGN SIZE 1 inch (25mm) square
STITCH COUNT 14 x 15

Zweigart white 14-count Aida
  2 x 2 inches (50 x 50mm)
White polyester sewing thread
Sharps size 10 needle
Tapestry size 24 needle
25cm jade or grape Offray ribbon, 1.5mm wide
Impress three-fold gift tag

BEADS

COLOUR	BEADESIGN	MILL HILL	BEADESIGN PACKETS
Sapphire blue	173	2006	One
Sapphire blue heart	C8		One
Hot pink	89	62035(F)	One
Quartz pink heart	C4		One

1 To stitch the design, begin by following the instructions given for the Valentine Card, see left.

2 Using the pattern for the large pink bead heart taken from the chart opposite, carefully work the design.

3 When the beadwork is complete, stitch the small heart to the bottom of the design at the point shown on the chart.

4 Mount the design following the instructions given on pages 112–14.

5 Finish the gift tag with the ribbon.

VICTORIAN CUPID SILHOUETTES

A mirror image of this charming cupid has been charted so that you can stitch a pair to frame either individually or together. They would make a romantic gift for someone special.

DESIGN SIZE 2¼ x 3¼ inches (56 x 81mm)
STITCH COUNT 38 x 46

Materials for each cupid:
Zweigart cream 14-count Aida
  5 x 6 inches (125 x 150mm)
Cream polyester sewing thread
Sharps size 10 needle
Framecraft 3½ x 4½ inches (88 x 113mm) oval, gold-coloured frame for mounting

BEADS

COLOUR	BEADESIGN	MILL HILL	BEADESIGN PACKETS
Black gold	75	221	Two

1 Find the centre of the material as described in Beginning a Project (page 14).

2 Stitch the cupid, following the chart on page 70.

3 Mount in the oval frame following the manufacturer's instructions.

Mother's Day

*T*HIS PRETTY DESIGN *makes an attractive card. A small picture, in matching colours, completes the gift. The designs are shown in two colourways. The stunning flowers on these mother's day cards and pictures have been stitched with beads, and there is a beautiful contrast between the beadwork flowers and the greenery.*

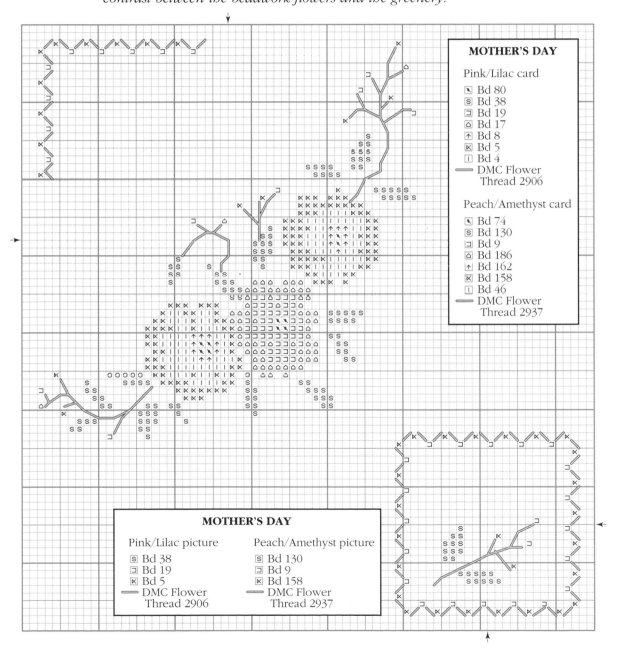

MOTHER'S DAY

Pink/Lilac card

- ◥ Bd 80
- ⑤ Bd 38
- ⊐ Bd 19
- ⬠ Bd 17
- ↑ Bd 8
- ⊠ Bd 5
- ⊥ Bd 4
- — DMC Flower Thread 2906

Peach/Amethyst card

- ◥ Bd 74
- ⑤ Bd 130
- ⊐ Bd 9
- ⬠ Bd 186
- ↑ Bd 162
- ⊠ Bd 158
- ⊥ Bd 46
- — DMC Flower Thread 2937

MOTHER'S DAY

Pink/Lilac picture	Peach/Amethyst picture
⑤ Bd 38	⑤ Bd 130
⊐ Bd 19	⊐ Bd 9
⊠ Bd 5	⊠ Bd 158
— DMC Flower Thread 2906	— DMC Flower Thread 2937

PINK/LILAC CARD

DESIGN SIZE 3¾ x 3¾ inches (94 x 94mm)
STITCH COUNT 51 x 52

Zweigart white 14-count Aida
  6 x 6 inches (150 x 150mm)
White polyester sewing thread
DMC flower thread 2906 for green back stitch
DMC flower thread 2899 for pink back stitch
Sharps size 10 needle
Tapestry size 24 needle
Impress large, square, white three-fold card for
mounting

BEADS

COLOUR	BEADESIGN	MILL HILL	BEADESIGN PACKETS
Mid yellow	80	2002	One
Emerald	38	167	One
Purple/blue	19	252	One
Medium lilac	17	2009	One
Clover pink	8	553	One
Medium pink	5	2005	One
Baby pink	4	145	One

1   Chart your chosen name or greeting from
the alphabets on pages 31 or 39.

2   Find the centre of the chart and the fabric
and mark the centre with a contrasting
thread as described in Beginning a Project
(page 14).

3   Stitch the design following the chart on page
73. The lettering, flower stems and parts of
the border are worked in back stitch, using
the flower thread and the tapestry needle.

4   Details for mounting the work in the card
are given on pages 112–13.

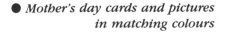

● *Mother's day cards and pictures
in matching colours*

PINK/LILAC PICTURE

DESIGN SIZE 1¾ x 1¾ inches (44 x 44mm)
STITCH COUNT 24 x 24

Zweigart white 14-count Aida
  2½ x 2½ inches (63 x 63mm)
White polyester sewing thread
DMC flower thread 2899 for pink back stitch
DMC flower thread 2906 for green back stitch
Sharps size 10 needle
Tapestry size 24 needle
25cm pink Offray ribbon, 1.5mm wide
DMC 2½ inch (63mm) square, gold frame for
mounting

BEADS

COLOUR	BEADESIGN	MILL HILL	BEADESIGN PACKETS
Emerald	38	167	One
Purple/blue	19	252	One
Medium pink	5	2005	One

1 Follow the stitching instructions given for the Pink/Lilac Card (page 74).

2 Finishing and mounting instructions are given on pages 112–14.

PEACH/AMETHYST CARD

DESIGN SIZE 3¾ x 3¾ inches (94 x 94mm)
STITCH COUNT 51 x 52

Zweigart cream 14-count Aida
  6 x 6 inches (150 x 150mm)
Cream polyester sewing thread
DMC flower thread 2937
Stranded cotton (embroidery floss) DMC
315/Madeira 0810
Sharps size 10 needle
Tapestry size 24 needle
Impress large, square, dusky pink three-fold card
for mounting

BEADS

COLOUR	BEADESIGN	MILL HILL	BEADESIGN PACKETS
Copper	74	330	One
Green iris	130	3022	One
Amethyst	9	3023(A)	One
Pale rose pink	186	3018	One
Pale pink	162	3005(A)	One
Soft peach	158	2003	One
Apricot	46	148	One

1 Follow the stitching and mounting instructions for the Pink/Lilac Card (page 74), but use two strands of cotton (floss) to back stitch 'MUM'.

PEACH/AMETHYST PICTURE

DESIGN SIZE 1¾ x 1¾ inches (44 x 44mm)
STITCH COUNT 24 x 24

Zweigart cream 14-count Aida
  2½ x 2½ inches (63 x 63mm)
Cream polyester sewing thread
DMC flower thread 2937
Stranded cotton (embroidery floss) DMC
315/Madeira 0810
Sharps size 10 needle
Tapestry size 24 needle
25cm peach Offray ribbon, 1.5mm wide
DMC 2½ inch (63mm) square, gold frame for
mounting

BEADS

COLOUR	BEADESIGN	MILL HILL	BEADESIGN PACKETS
Green iris	130	3022	One
Amethyst	9	3023(A)	One
Soft peach	158	2003	One

1 Follow the stitching and mounting instructions for the Pink/Lilac Picture (above left), using two strands of cotton (floss) for the lettering.

Father's Day

*T*HIS DESIGN *was inspired by an embroidery pattern found on an antique linen sampler. This kind of pattern would have been worked in only one or two colours. The simple design uses colour to produce a bold, striking pattern to stitch as a card or penholder.*

FATHER'S DAY CARD

DESIGN SIZE 2¼ x 2¼ inches (56 x 56mm)
STITCH COUNT 31 x 31

Blue Fiddlers cloth 14-count
  3½ x 4 inches (88 x 100mm)
Matching polyester sewing thread
DMC flower thread 2346
Sharps size 10 needle
Tapestry size 24 needle
Craft Creations card with 2½ inch (63mm) diameter aperture, bright red with gold foil borderline, for mounting

BEADS

COLOUR	BEADESIGN	MILL HILL	BEADESIGN PACKETS
Ultra marine	169	358	One
Plum	10	2012	One

1   To stitch the card, begin by finding the centre of the fabric as described in Beginning a Project (page 14).

2   Following the chart above right, stitch the design in your chosen colourway.

3   Back stitch 'DAD' using the flower thread and tapestry needle, and following the alphabet chart on pages 31 and 39.

4   Instructions for finishing and mounting are given on pages 112–14.

FATHER'S DAY PENHOLDER

DESIGN SIZE 2¼ x 2¼ inches (56 x 56mm)
STITCH COUNT 31 x 31

Zweigart rustico 14-count Aida
  3½ x 4 inches (88 x 100mm)
Matching polyester sewing thread
DMC flower thread 2666

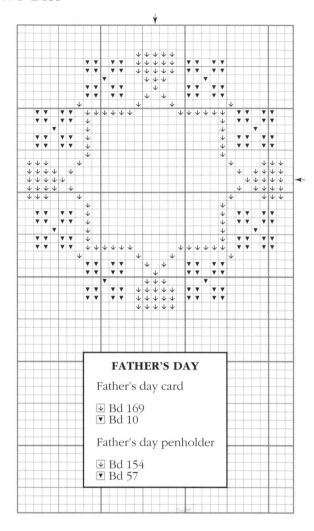

FATHER'S DAY

Father's day card

↓ Bd 169
▼ Bd 10

Father's day penholder

↓ Bd 154
▼ Bd 57

Sharps size 10 needle
Tapestry size 24 needle
Framecraft wood desk kit 2⅝ inches (63mm) round

BEADS

COLOUR	BEADESIGN	MILL HILL	BEADESIGN PACKETS
Moss green	154	3037	One
Christmas red	57	2013	One

1   Following the instructions for making the Father's Day Card, carefully stitch the design.

2   Mount the design in the penholder by following the manufacturer's instructions.

Easter

THESE CHARMING DUCKS and ducklings would make a welcome addition to a child's bedroom wall at any time of year. They are easy to stitch and would also make attractive Easter cards.

The Easter eggs are intended for the reader to use as a design library. Four of them have been used to make an attractive Easter card stitched on 18-count Aida and using miniature beads. Alternatively, they could be worked on 14-count Aida or stitching paper using 11/0 beads. Use stitching paper to make gift tags or decorations.

DUCK WITH EASTER BONNET

DESIGN SIZE 2¼ x 3¼ inches (56 x 81mm)
STITCH COUNT 31 x 46

Zweigart lemon 14-count Aida
  6 x 7 inches (150 x 175mm)
Lemon polyester sewing thread
DMC flower thread 2730, 2734
Sharps size 10 needle
Tapestry size 24 needle
DMC Georgian 5 x 7 inches (125 x 175mm) frame
for mounting

BEADS

COLOUR	BEADESIGN	MILL HILL	BEADESIGN PACKETS
Mid grey	62	283	One
White	2	479	One
Aqua blue	26	2007	One
Sky blue	170	2017	One
Turquoise	109	62038(F)	One
Tangerine	118	165	One
Light tangerine	51	423	One
Black	78	2014	One

1 Find the centre of the fabric as described in Beginning a Project (page 14) and start stitching from the centre following the chart on page 82.

2 The nest is worked in cross stitch using the flower thread and the tapestry needle.

3 Instructions for finishing and mounting are given on pages 112–14.

EASTER DUCKLINGS

WALKING DUCKLING

DESIGN SIZE 2½ x 2¼ inches (62 x 58mm)
STITCH COUNT 34 x 32

PECKING DUCKLING

DESIGN SIZE 2¼ x 2 inches (58 x 53mm)
STITCH COUNT 34 x 29

For either design:
Zweigart cream 14-count Aida
  6 x 6 inches (150 x 150mm)
Cream polyester sewing thread
Stranded cotton (embroidery floss) DMC 947/Madeira 0205
Sharps size 10 needle
Tapestry size 24 needle
Kraftie Kits small, pine frame 3¾ x 4¾ inches (92 x 119mm) for mounting

BEADS

COLOUR	BEADESIGN	MILL HILL	BEADESIGN PACKETS
Daffodil	140	62041(F)	One
Tangerine	50	423	One
Dark emerald	42	332	One
Black	78	2014	One

1 Find the centre of the fabric as described in Beginning a Project (page 14), and start stitching from the centre, following the chart on page 82.

2 Back stitch 'Happy Easter' if required, using two strands of cotton (floss) in the tapestry needle and following the alphabet chart on pages 31 and 39.

3 The position of the bow is marked on the chart at the neckline. Work the bow using six strands of cotton (floss).

4 Instructions for finishing and mounting are given on pages 112–14. Alternatively, these ducklings would also make an ideal Easter card.

● *Opposite: Easter ducklings*

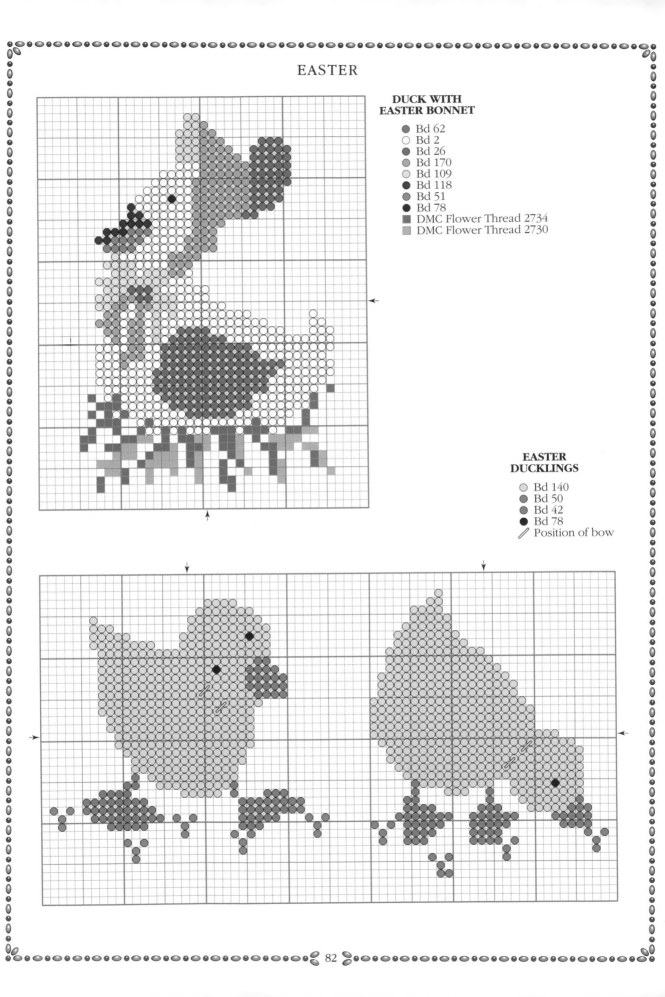

DUCK WITH EASTER BONNET

- ● Bd 62
- ○ Bd 2
- ● Bd 26
- ● Bd 170
- ○ Bd 109
- ● Bd 118
- ● Bd 51
- ● Bd 78
- ■ DMC Flower Thread 2734
- ■ DMC Flower Thread 2730

EASTER DUCKLINGS

- ○ Bd 140
- ● Bd 50
- ● Bd 42
- ● Bd 78
- ⫽ Position of bow

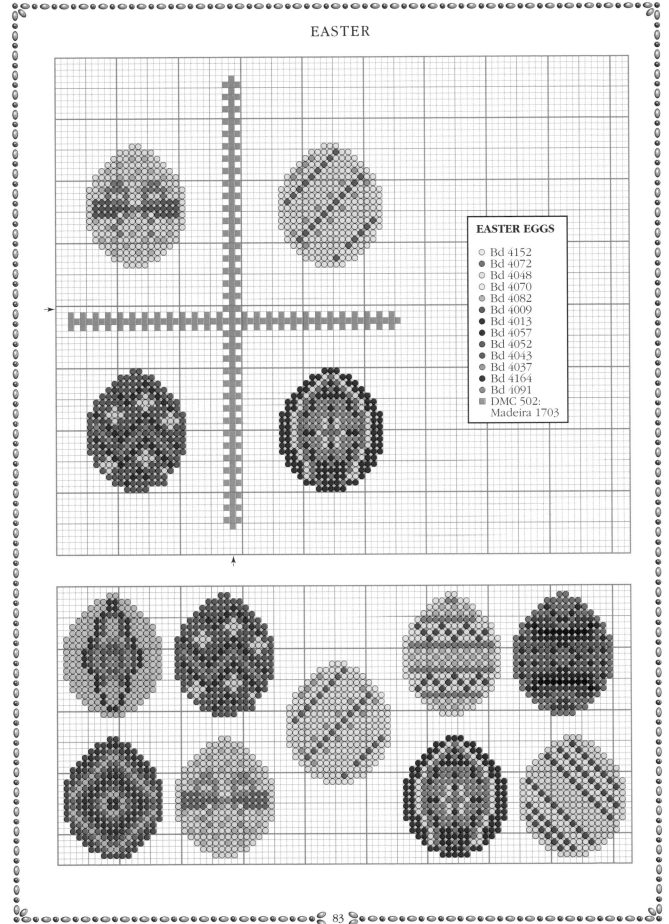

EASTER EGGS

- ○ Bd 4152
- ● Bd 4072
- ○ Bd 4048
- ○ Bd 4070
- ● Bd 4082
- ● Bd 4009
- ● Bd 4013
- ● Bd 4057
- ● Bd 4052
- ● Bd 4043
- ● Bd 4037
- ● Bd 4164
- ● Bd 4091
- ■ DMC 502:
  Madeira 1703

EASTER EGGS CARD

DESIGN SIZE 3 x 4 inches (75 x 100mm)
STITCH COUNT 54 x 73

Zweigart cream 18-count Aida
  5 x 6 inches (125 x 150mm)
Cream polyester sewing thread
Stranded cotton (embroidery floss) DMC
502/Madeira 1703
Beading needle
Tapestry size 24 needle
From Craft Creations:
Yellow cord with tassels
Easter greeting paper motif
Plain, cream 6 x 8 inches (150 x 200mm) oblong
card with 3 x 4 inches (75 x 100mm) aperture

BEADS

COLOUR	BEADESIGN	MILL HILL	BEADESIGN PACKETS
Cream	4152	40123	One
Antique gold	4072	40557	One
Yellow	4048	42011	One
Gold	4070	42011	One
Duck egg blue	4082	42017	One
Amethyst	4009	42024	One
Wine	4013	40374	One
Christmas red	4057	42028	One
Burnt orange	4052	42013	One
Antique green	4043	45270	One
Emerald	4037	40332	One
Deep lilac	4164	40252	One
Deep dusty pink	4091	42024	One

1 Begin by finding the centre of the fabric as described in Beginning a Project (page 14).

2 Stitch the dividing lines in cross stitch using one strand of stranded cotton (embroidery floss) in the tapestry needle.

3 Stitch the Easter eggs by following the chart on page 83.

4 Mount your work in the card following the instructions given on pages 112–14. Decorate the card with the tassel and paper motif.

Christmas

●●●●●●●●●●●●●●● ✻ ✻ ●●●●●●●●●●●●●●●

Cʜʀɪsᴛᴍᴀs is such a special time of year. Delight your family and friends by making them cards or sparkling decorations for the tree. All the designs are quick and easy to make and will bring lasting pleasure.

FIR TREE CARD

ᴅᴇsɪɢɴ sɪᴢᴇ 1½ x 2¼ inches (38 x 56mm)
sᴛɪᴛᴄʜ ᴄᴏᴜɴᴛ 21 x 32

Charles Craft navy 14-count Aida
  4 x 4 inches (100 x 100mm)
Navy polyester sewing thread
Sharps size 10 needle
Impress silver card with 3 inch (75mm) diameter aperture

BEADS

COLOUR	BEADESIGN	MILL HILL	BEADESIGN PACKETS
Silver rainbow	145	2010	One
White	2	479	One
White	137	3015(A)	One

1   Begin by finding the centre of the material as described in Beginning a Project (page 14).

2   Attach the beads carefully, following the chart on page 89.

3   Instructions for mounting into cards are given on pages 112–13.

● *A variety of Christmas cards illustrating the traditional fir tree, church, robin and holly wreath*

CHURCH CARD

DESIGN SIZE 2 x 2 inches (50 x 50mm)
STITCH COUNT 28 x 26

Charles Craft navy 14-count Aida
  4 x 4 inches (100 x 100mm)
Navy polyester sewing thread
Sharps size 10 needle
Impress silver card with 3 inch (75mm) diameter aperture

BEADS

COLOUR	BEADESIGN	MILL HILL	BEADESIGN PACKETS
Silver rainbow	145	2010	One
White	2	479	One
White	137	3015A	One
Gold rainbow	143	2011	One

1 Follow the instructions given for the Fir Tree Card on page 86.

ROBIN CARD

DESIGN SIZE 1½ x 1½ inches (38 x 38mm)
STITCH COUNT 22 x 20

Zweigart cream 14-count Aida
  3 x 3 inches (75 x 75mm)
Cream polyester sewing thread
Stranded cotton (embroidery floss) DMC 433/Madeira 2008
Sharps size 10 needle
Tapestry size 24 needle
Craft Creations Christmas greeting card with 2¼ inch (63mm) diameter aperture

BEADS

COLOUR	BEADESIGN	MILL HILL	BEADESIGN PACKETS
Brown	76	2023	One
Christmas red	57	2013	One
Dark emerald	42	332	One
Deep black	65	3026	One

1 Follow the stitching instructions for the Fir Tree Card on page 86, but in addition, back stitch the robin's beak and feet using two strands of cotton (floss) in the tapestry needle when the beadwork is complete.

2 Mount the design in the card, following the instructions on pages 112–13 or, alternatively, mount in a 2¼ inch (63mm) diameter frame or flexi-hoop, and use as a tree decoration.

HOLLY WREATH CARD

DESIGN SIZE 2 x 2¼ inches (50 x 56mm)
STITCH COUNT 27 x 33

Zweigart white 14-count Aida
  3½ x 3½ inches (88 x 88mm)
White polyester sewing thread
Sharps size 10 needle
Craft Creations Christmas greeting card with 2¾ inch (69mm) diameter aperture

BEADS

COLOUR	BEADESIGN	MILL HILL	BEADESIGN PACKETS
Antique gold	72	557	One
Bright gold	70	2011	One
Christmas red	56	2013	One
Dark emerald	40	2020	One
Dark emerald	41	2020	One

1 Follow the instructions given for the Fir Tree Card on page 86.

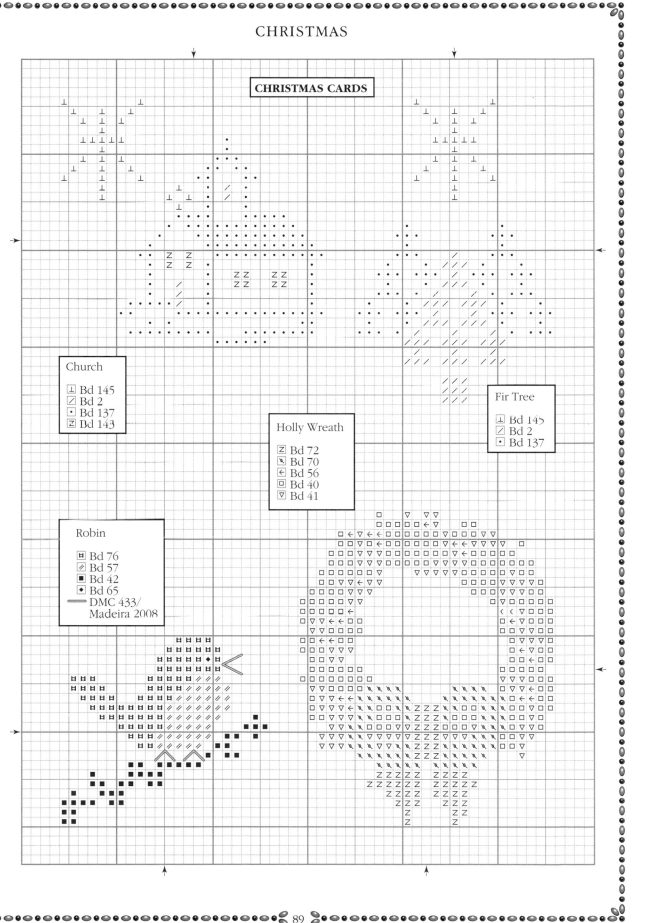

CHRISTMAS CARDS

Church

⊥ Bd 145
⧄ Bd 2
• Bd 137
ℤ Bd 143

Holly Wreath

ℤ Bd 72
◥ Bd 70
← Bd 56
□ Bd 40
▽ Bd 41

Fir Tree

⊥ Bd 145
⧄ Bd 2
• Bd 137

Robin

H Bd 76
⧄ Bd 57
■ Bd 42
◆ Bd 65
— DMC 433/
Madeira 2008

PLAYFUL PENGUIN CHRISTMAS CARDS

These attractive penguins, in their various poses and hats, would make delightful Christmas cards for children. The stripes on the hats are intended to be changed to vary the designs. Details of all the colours used for the hats are given in the materials list so that the penguins can be stitched as photographed if desired.

The designs were mounted in a selection of small cards from Craft Creations and Kraftie Kits.

PENGUINS IN RED OR GREEN HATS
DESIGN SIZE 1½ x 1¾ inches (38 x 44mm)
STITCH COUNT 20 x 26

PENGUINS IN BLUE, PURPLE OR GOLD HATS
DESIGN SIZE 1¼ x 2 inches (31 x 50mm)
STITCH COUNT 17 x 29

Materials for all penguins
Jane Greenoff's mid blue stitching paper
3 x 3 inches (75 x 75mm)
Mid blue polyester sewing thread
Sharps size 10 needle

BEADS

COLOUR	BEADESIGN	MILL HILL	BEADESIGN PACKETS
Rainbow white	1	161	One
White	2	479	One
Deep black	65	3026	One
Sapphire	166	2006	One
Bright gold	70	2011	One
Aqua/purple	151	252	One
Christmas red	57	2013	One
Christmas red	56	2013	One
Tangerine	50	423	One
Emerald	37	62049(F)	One
Blue rainbow	147	2026	One
Black	78	2014	One

● *The playful penguin Christmas card, also incorporated into a gift tag, and penguin box lid*

1 Stitch your chosen design by following the chart and using two strands of thread for extra security.

2 When using double-sided tape to mount stitching paper into cards, back your design with either another piece of stitching paper or a piece of plain paper of the same colour. This will prevent the tape from showing through. Additional instructions for mounting into cards are given on pages 112–13.

ALTERNATIVES

1 When the design is complete, back it with a piece of stitching paper and carefully cut round the penguin one hole away from the beads. Add an attractive thread to the top and hang him on your tree or on a present as a gift tag.

2 Stitch the beads on Charles Craft ridge blue 14-count Aida 5 x 5 inches (125 x 125mm). Back stitch round the hat using DMC 310/Madeira black stranded cotton (embroidery floss), using two strands. Mount in DMC 3 inch (75mm) red flexi-hoop and use as a tree decoration or small Christmas picture for a child.

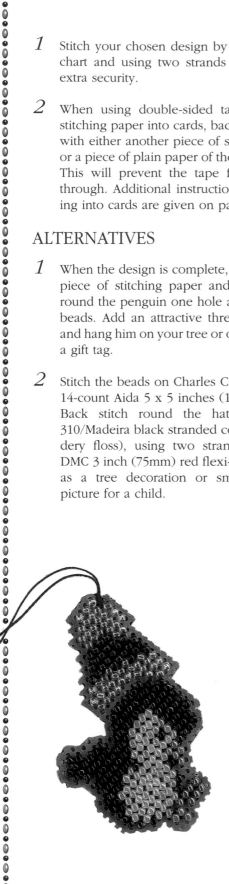

PENGUIN BOX LID

This charming penguin is mounted in the lid of a red enamel box. You could fill the box with a Christmas surprise and give it to a friend or relative.

DESIGN SIZE 2 x 2¼ inches (50 x 56mm)
STITCH COUNT 27 x 31

Charles Craft pale blue 14-count Aida
  6 x 6 inches (150 x 150mm)
Pale blue polyester sewing thread
Stranded cotton (embroidery floss) DMC 310/Madeira black
Sharps size 10 needle
Tapestry size 24 needle
Framecraft 3½ inch (88mm) diameter red enamel box

BEADS

COLOUR	BEADESIGN	MILL HILL	BEADESIGN PACKETS
Rainbow white	1	161	One
White	2	479	One
Deep black	65	3026	One
Sapphire	166	2006	One
Christmas red	56	2013	One
Tangerine	50	423	One
Black	78	2014	One

1 Begin by finding the centre of the material as described in Beginning a Project (page 14).

2 Stitch the design following the chart on page 93.

3 Using two strands of cotton (floss) and the tapestry needle, back stitch around the hat as shown on the chart.

4 Mount the design in the box lid following the manufacturer's instructions, but do not cover the beads with the acetate disc as it may distort them.

● *Use as a gift tag or a tree decoration*

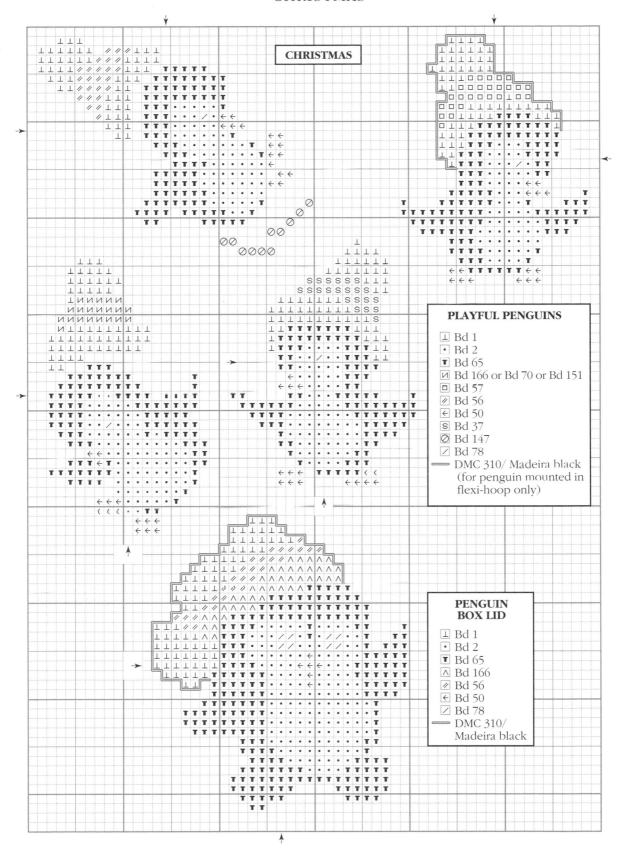

CHRISTMAS

PLAYFUL PENGUINS

⊥ Bd 1
• Bd 2
T Bd 65
И Bd 166 or Bd 70 or Bd 151
▢ Bd 57
⊘ Bd 56
← Bd 50
S Bd 37
⊘ Bd 147
⟋ Bd 78
— DMC 310/ Madeira black
(for penguin mounted in
flexi-hoop only)

PENGUIN BOX LID

⊥ Bd 1
• Bd 2
T Bd 65
∧ Bd 166
⊘ Bd 56
← Bd 50
⟋ Bd 78
— DMC 310/
Madeira black

CHRISTMAS STOCKING

Everyone likes to have a Christmas stocking. These are available in red or green, and would delight both children and adults. You could add a name in back stitch using the alphabet charts on pages 31 and 39 to make a special, personalised stocking.

Christmas stocking with 14-count Aida
   band, from Wimble Bees (see stockist list)
White polyester sewing thread
Sharps size 10 needle

BEADS

COLOUR	BEADESIGN	MILL HILL	BEADESIGN PACKETS
Assorted silver lined beads to be used at random for the tree lights			
Dark emerald	42	332	One

1 Attach the green beads following the chart opposite.

2 Add the silver lined beads at random to give the desired effect.

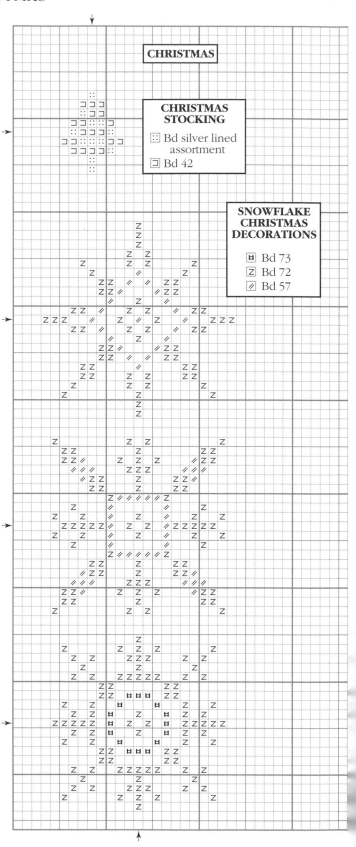

CHRISTMAS

CHRISTMAS STOCKING
- :: Bd silver lined assortment
- ⊐ Bd 42

SNOWFLAKE CHRISTMAS DECORATIONS
- H Bd 73
- Z Bd 72
- ⁄ Bd 57

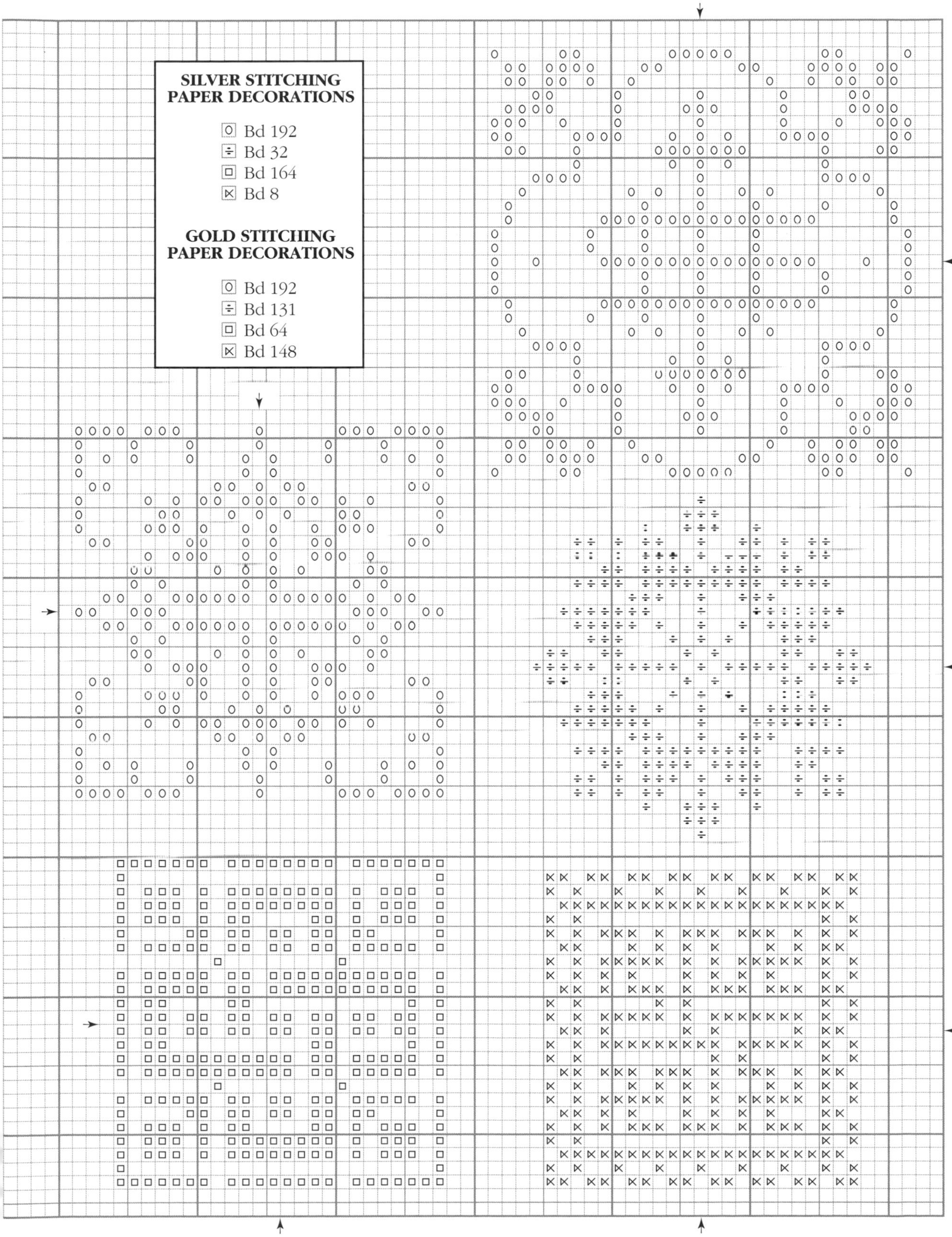

SILVER STITCHING PAPER DECORATIONS

- ○ Bd 192
- ÷ Bd 32
- ☐ Bd 164
- ☒ Bd 8

GOLD STITCHING PAPER DECORATIONS

- ○ Bd 192
- ÷ Bd 131
- ☐ Bd 64
- ☒ Bd 148

SNOWFLAKE CHRISTMAS DECORATIONS

These simple designs will add a little sparkle to your tree. They are quick and easy to stitch and could be worked on any colour of 14-count Aida then mounted into cards.

DESIGN SIZES 1½ x 1½ inches (38 x 38mm) and 1¼ x 1¼ inches (31 x 31mm)
STITCH COUNTS 21 x 21 (green) and 19 x 19 (blue and red)

● The snowflake, shown in detail above, is just one of the sparkling decorations to make for the Christmas tree (pages 96-7)

Zweigart holly green 14-count Aida or
Charles Craft navy 14-count Aida or
Zweigart Christmas red 14-count Aida
   4 x 4 inches (100 x 100mm)
Matching polyester sewing thread
Sharps size 10 needle
Oddment of ribbon for hanging the decoration if required
DMC 2¼ inch (63mm) diameter gold frame

BEADS

COLOUR	BEADESIGN	MILL HILL	BEADESIGN PACKETS
Bronze	73	221	One
Antique gold	72	557	One
Christmas red	57	2013	One

1 To stitch any of the decorations, begin by finding the centre of the fabric as described in Beginning a Project (page 14).

2 Work the design following the chart on pages 94–5.

3 To mount the snowflakes, use the clear acetate cover from the frame as a template by placing it centrally over the design and drawing round it with a pencil.

4 Cut away the excess fabric. Cut a piece of wadding (batting) to the same size as the fabric.

5 Place the design and the wadding (batting) in the frame and replace the backing. Do not cover the beads with the acetate disc as it may distort them.

TREE DECORATIONS USING STITCHING/PERFORATED PAPER

BRIGHT JADE DECORATIONS
DESIGN SIZE 2¼ x 2¼ inches (57 x 57mm)
STITCH COUNT 31 x 31

DESIGN SIZE 2 x 2 inches (49 x 49mm)
STITCH COUNT 27 x 27

Jane Greenoff's gold or silver stitching paper
  3 x 3 inches (75 x 75mm) or Perforated
  paper from Wimble Bees
Polyester sewing thread, cream for gold paper,
white for silver
Sharps size 10 needle
Oddment of metallic thread for hanging

BEADS

COLOUR	BEADESIGN	MILL HILL	BEADESIGN PACKETS
Bright jade	192	62038(F)	One
Light green	32	561	One
Ruby/gold	131	3033	One
Deep lilac	164	62042(F)	One
Rainbow black	64	374	One
Clover pink	8	553	One
Aqua rainbow	148	3035	One

These five designs use beads in a variety of colours and are shown worked on gold and silver stitching papers. Alternatively, you could use your own choice of colours.

CLOVER PINK OR AQUA RAINBOW DECORATION
DESIGN SIZE 1⅔ x 1⅔ inches (42 x 42mm)
STITCH COUNT 23 x 23

LIGHT GREEN OR RUBY/GOLD DECORATION
DESIGN SIZE 1¾ x 1¾ inches (44 x 44mm)
STITCH COUNT 25 x 25

DEEP LILAC OR RAINBOW BLACK DECORATION
DESIGN SIZE 1¾ x 1¾ inches (44 x 44mm)
STITCH COUNT 24 x 24

1 To stitch any of these decorations, begin by finding the centre of the paper (see page 14).

2 Work the design by following the chart on pages 94–5 and using two strands of thread for extra security.

3 Trim away the excess paper leaving a margin of one hole all the way round the design.

4 Back the decoration using stitching paper, or plain paper, to hide the threads.

5 Trim off the corners if required. Attach thread to make a hanging loop.

Bead Geometrics

BEADS lend themselves beautifully to geometric designs, as shown in this candlescreen and glasses case.

The design for the unusual glasses case was inspired by a pattern on an Egyptian tile. The colours chosen reflect the original colours on the tile, but you can adapt them to co-ordinate with your own colour scheme. The design is a repeating pattern and can be extended or reduced to fit a larger or smaller design area. You could, for example, use the design to good effect for a needlecase or purse.

CANDLESCREEN

DESIGN SIZE 3 x 3 inches (75 x 75mm)
STITCH COUNT 43 x 43

Zweigart black 14-count Aida
  6 x 6 inches (150 x 150mm)
Black polyester sewing thread
Sharps size 10 needle
Candlescreen, 15 inches (375mm) high, in yew finish, from Market Square (see list of suppliers page 119)

BEADS

COLOUR	BEADESIGN	MILL HILL	BEADESIGN PACKETS
Antique gold	72	557	Two

1 Find the centre of the material as described in Beginning a Project (page 14). Begin stitching from the centre of the chart on the right.

2 Mount your finished design in the candlescreen following the manufacturer's instructions.

ALTERNATIVES

1 Add a mount, and frame as a conventional picture.

2 Work the design in a bright colour on white or cream fabric and mount in a brightly coloured frame.

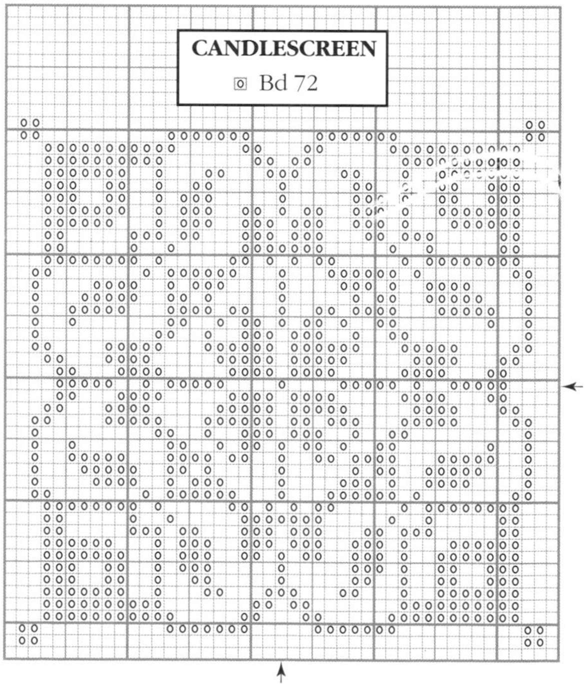

CANDLESCREEN
◎ Bd 72

GLASSES CASE

DESIGN SIZE $7\frac{1}{2}$ x $2\frac{3}{4}$ inches (188 x 69mm)
STITCH COUNT 103 x 39

Zweigart cream 14-count Aida
  18 x 6 inches (450 x 150mm)
Cream polyester sewing thread
Sharps size 10 needle
Remnant of cotton fabric for the lining
  18 x 4 inches (450 x 100mm)

BEADS

COLOUR	BEADESIGN	MILL HILL	BEADESIGN PACKETS
Black	78	2014	One
Cream	152	123	One
Ultra marine	169	358	Two
Deep orange	161	165	One
Moss green	154	3037	Two

1 Begin by folding the fabric in half width-ways. Mark the foldline with a row of running stitches in a contrasting colour. One half of the material will be for the front of the case and will be decorated with the beads, the second half will be for the back and can be left unstitched. If you decide to stitch the design on both the back and the front of the case, you will need to buy twice as many beads.

2 In a different coloured thread, stitch another row of running stitches, two squares up from the first row. This marks the point where the design finishes.

3 Find the centre of the design area following the instructions in Beginning a Project (page 14).

4 Stitch the design following the chart on the right.

5 When the work is complete, fold the material along the centre line of running stitches, with the design to the inside.

6 Back stitch or machine stitch the two long sides together, two squares from the edge of the design.

7 Trim the excess material to within two squares of this line of stitching.

8 Trim the material at the front edge so that eight squares of fabric remain. Fold six squares to the inside of the case and slip stitch all the way round.

9 Turn the case right side out.

TO MAKE THE LINING:

1 Cut the lining material to the same size as the finished case and fold it in half widthways with the right side inside.

2 Machine or back stitch the two long sides together so that the width of the lining is equal to the width of the design.

3 Trim the seams to approximately ¼ inch (7mm). Do not turn the lining.

4 Slip the lining into the case, making sure that the bottom corners fit neatly into the corners.

5 Stitch the lining to the case at each corner with two back stitches to hold it firmly in place, using cream thread.

6 Trim the front edge of the lining so that it is approximately ¼ inch (7mm) longer than the case.

7 Turn this excess fabric in, and back stitch or hem stitch it neatly to the case.

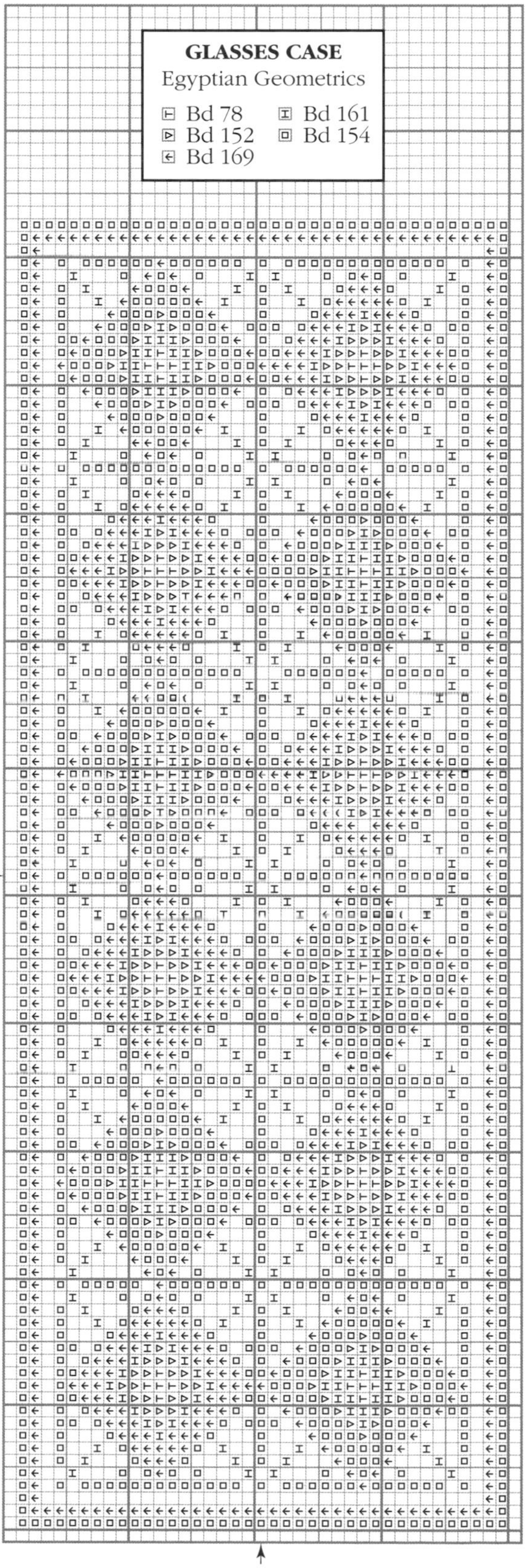

GLASSES CASE
Egyptian Geometrics

⊞ Bd 78   ⊠ Bd 161
▷ Bd 152   ▣ Bd 154
⊡ Bd 169

Sampler Motif Trinket Boxes

*T*HESE THREE DESIGNS *are based on traditional motifs used on samplers over the centuries. The boxes are available in a variety of colours, sizes and shapes. By choosing your favourite colour and using co-ordinating beads, you can give your box lid a personal touch.*

SMALL ROUND BOX LID

DESIGN SIZE 2 x 2 inches (50 x 50mm)
STITCH COUNT 27 x 27

Charles Craft very pale-blue 14-count Aida
   3½ x 3½ inches (88 x 88mm)
Very pale-blue polyester sewing thread
Kreinik metallic fine (#8) braid 9294
Sharps size 10 needle
Tapestry size 24 needle
Framecraft 2⅝ inch (66mm) diameter, blue porcelain box

BEADS

COLOUR	BEADESIGN	MILL HILL	BEADESIGN PACKETS
French navy	194	60168(F)	One
Blue/purple	102	252	One

1 Begin by finding the centre of the material as described in Beginning a Project (page 14).

2 Apply the beads following the chart on page 106 and then add the back stitch using the metallic braid and the tapestry needle.

3 Mount the design following the manufacturer's instructions, but do not use the acetate disc to cover the beads as it will distort them. Instead, use it as extra backing to hold your work firmly in place.

LARGE ROUND BOX LID

DESIGN SIZE 3 x 3 inches (75 x 75mm)
STITCH COUNT 42 x 42

Zweigart antique-white 14-count Aida
   4 x 4 inches (100 x 100mm)
Off-white polyester sewing thread
Sharps size 10 needle
Framecraft 3½ inch (88mm) diameter, blush porcelain box

BEADS

COLOUR	BEADESIGN	MILL HILL	BEADESIGN PACKETS
Wine	13	3033	One
Clover pink	96	2024	One
Deep dusty pink	91	3019	One

1 Stitch the design following the instructions for the Small Round Box Lid left but omit the back stitching.

2 Mount the design following the manufacturer's instructions, but do not cover the beads with the acetate disc as it may distort them.

● *Trinket boxes in a variety of shapes and sizes*

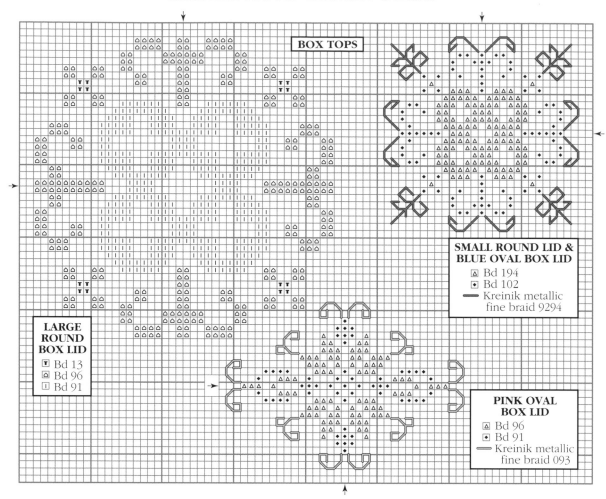

BOX TOPS

**SMALL ROUND LID &
BLUE OVAL BOX LID**
⊠ Bd 194
◆ Bd 102
— Kreinik metallic
fine braid 9294

**LARGE
ROUND
BOX LID**
T Bd 13
⊠ Bd 96
▯ Bd 91

**PINK OVAL
BOX LID**
⊠ Bd 96
◆ Bd 91
— Kreinik metallic
fine braid 093

BLUE OVAL BOX LID

DESIGN SIZE 2¼ x 1¾ inches (56 x 44mm)
STITCH COUNT 33 x 24

Charles Craft very pale-blue 14-count Aida
3½ x 3 inches (88 x 75mm)
Framecraft 2⅞ x 2 inches (72 x 50mm), blue oval
porcelain box

For beads and sewing requirements, refer to the
materials list given for the Small Round Box Lid
on page 104.

Stitching and mounting instructions are also as
for the Small Round Box Lid.

PINK OVAL BOX LID

DESIGN SIZE 2¼ x 1¾ inches (56 x 44mm)
STITCH COUNT 33 x 24

Zweigart antique-white 14-count Aida
3½ x 3 inches (88 x 75mm)
Off-white polyester sewing thread
Kreinik metallic fine (#8) braid 093
Sharps size 10 needle
Tapestry size 24 needle
Framecraft 2⅞ x 2 inches (72 x 50mm), blush oval
porcelain box

BEADS

COLOUR	BEADESIGN	MILL HILL	BEADESIGN PACKETS
Clover pink	96	2024	One
Deep dusty pink	91	3019	One

For stitching and mounting instructions, follow
those given for the Small Round Box Lid, page
104.

Borders

*A*N APPROPRIATE BORDER *will enhance a piece of work, complementing the original design without overpowering it. For example, the border on the 'Simon' name plaque on page 25 uses the same colours as the main design to bring the whole piece together and make an attractive picture.*

The borders shown in the Borders Sampler are a selection of modern and traditional styles for you to use as a design library, either to reproduce as shown or to alter as required. Colours have been suggested, but there are many more possibilities and you can adapt them according to your personal preference. When planning a border, there are several steps to follow before you begin stitching.

1 Begin by deciding what size the border needs to be. Plot this on graph paper, preferably using paper with the same number of squares (stitches) to the inch as your fabric, such as Design Sheets available from Craft Creations.

2 To check that the border design really fits the space available, identify the pattern repeat and the corner pattern segment. Copy the corner pattern segment on to the graph paper, positioning three of the corners as needed to border your design, so that you can count the number of squares between the corner segments, across the width and height.

3 Count the number of squares (stitches) between the corner pattern segments and the number of stitches in each pattern repeat. It will not normally be possible to insert a number of complete patterns into the space available, so it will be necessary to adapt the border pattern. Do this by adding one or more small elements taken from another border, or by altering the pattern, until the border fits.

4 Choose colours that complement the main design, perhaps using some of the same colours. Be careful not to overpower your original work with a border which is too strong in colour.

5 Calculate the number of beads needed for the whole border so that you can purchase all your beads at the same time, as dye lots do vary.

● *Border photograph frame (see page 111)*

BORDERS SAMPLER

This sampler is a library of patterns for borders, choose a border which suits the style of your work.

DESIGN SIZE 7 x 8¾ inches (175 x 219mm)
STITCH COUNT 99 x 122

Zweigart white 14-count Aida
   11 x 13 inches (275 x 325mm)
White polyester sewing thread
Sharps size 10 needle

BEADS

BORDER NO.	COLOUR	BEADESIGN	MILL HILL	BEADESIGN PACKETS
1	Baby blue	22	146	One
	Mid blue	23	168	One
2	Deep lilac	164	62042(F)	One
	Medium lilac	17	2009	One
3	Bronze	73	221	One
	Olive	122	62057(F)	One
4	Deep yellow	48	128	One
	Daffodil	140	62041(F)	One
	Deep jade	187	2021	One
5	Dusty sapphire	106	02015	One
	Aqua	107	62043(F)	One
6	Light ruby	93	2024	One
	Deep amethyst	94	2025	One
7	Christmas red	57	2013	One
	Deep yellow	48	128	One
	Emerald	37	62049(F)	One
	Royal blue	27	0020	One
8	Green/Grey	112	332	One
	Rose pink	6	2004	One
9	Clover pink	8	553	One
	Antique silver	68	3008	One
10	Deep ruby	95	3033	One
	Rose coral	49	2003	One
	Dark emerald	42	332	One
11	Light green	31	525	One
	Palest green	110	161	One
12	Sea green	138	2015	One
	Emerald	139	3028	One
13	Christmas red	57	2013	One
	Royal blue	27	0020	One
14	Plum	10	2012	One
	Rose pink	6	2004	One
	Dark emerald	42	332	One
15	Darkest green	160	2020	One

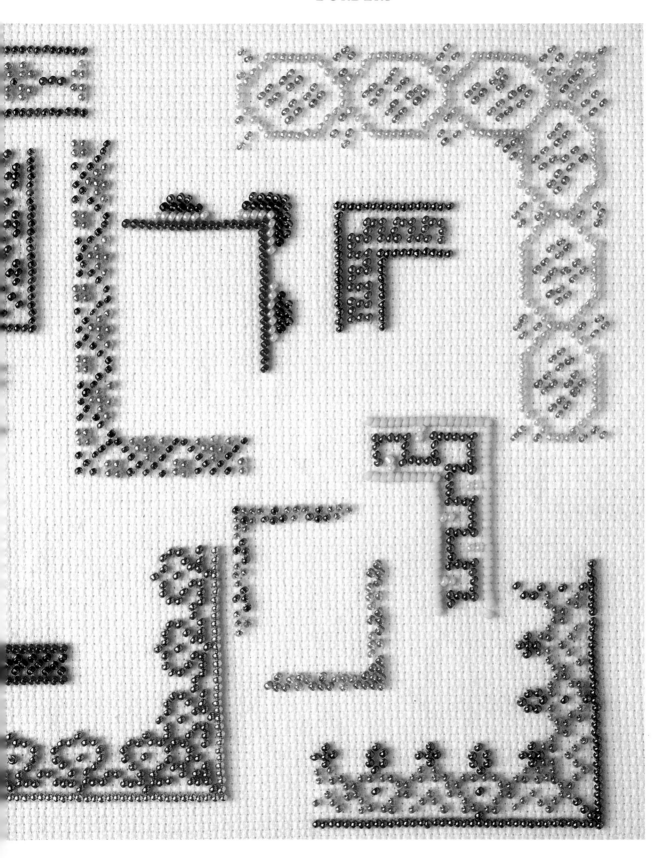

BORDERS

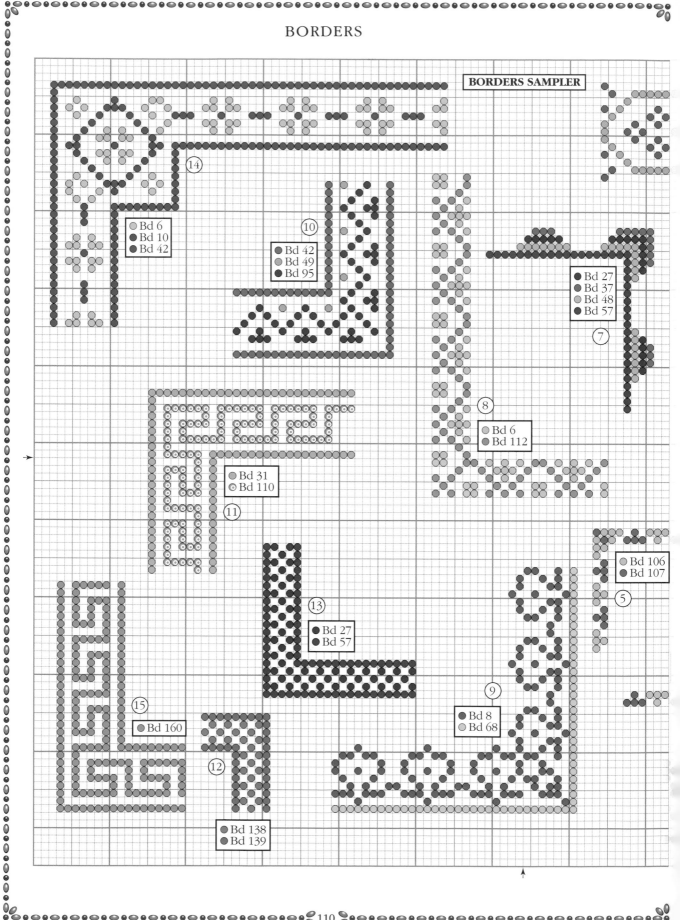

BORDERS SAMPLER

○ Bd 6
● Bd 10
● Bd 42

(14)

(10)
● Bd 42
○ Bd 49
● Bd 95

● Bd 27
● Bd 37
○ Bd 48
● Bd 57

(7)

(8)
● Bd 6
● Bd 112

● Bd 31
◎ Bd 110

(11)

● Bd 106
● Bd 107

(5)

(13)
● Bd 27
● Bd 57

(9)
● Bd 8
○ Bd 68

(15)
● Bd 160

(12)

● Bd 138
● Bd 139

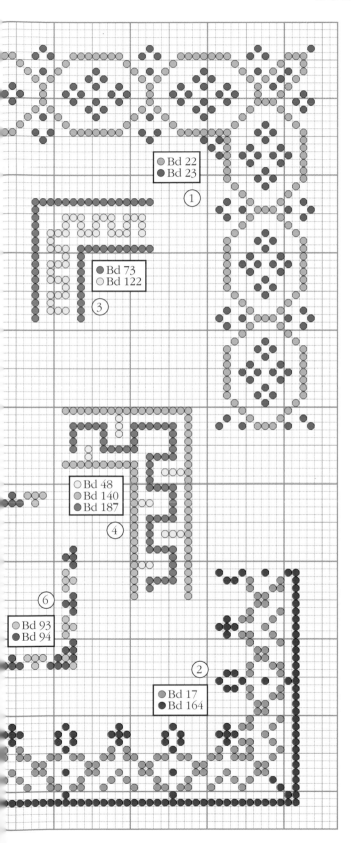

Bd 22
Bd 23
①

Bd 73
Bd 122
③

Bd 48
Bd 140
Bd 187
④

⑥

Bd 93
Bd 94

②

Bd 17
Bd 164

1 To stitch the sampler, begin by finding the centre of the material as described in Beginning a Project (page 14).

2 Working outward from the centre, stitch the borders following the chart opposite.

3 Mount and frame the sampler following the instructions on pages 112–14.

BORDER PHOTOGRAPH FRAME

This dainty photograph frame has been stitched to show how a simple border (number 5 from the Borders Sampler) can be used to good effect. Stitched in blue, or pink, it would make a delightful gift for a new mum to display baby's first photograph.

DESIGN SIZE 3 x 3¾ inches (75 x 94mm)
STITCH COUNT 42 x 53

Zweigart pale-blue 14-count Aida
  5 x 6 inches (125 x 150mm)
Pale blue polyester sewing thread
Sharps size 10 needle
Wadding (batting)
Fabric remnant in a contrasting colour
Craft Creations photograph frame 3½ x 4½ inches (88 x 113mm) with oblong aperture 2 x 3 inches (50 x 75mm)

BEADS

COLOUR	BEADESIGN	MILL HILL	BEADESIGN PACKETS
Dusty sapphire	106	2015	One
Aqua	107	62043(F)	One

1 To stitch and mount the photograph frame, carefully follow the instructions given for the Photograph Frame on page 21.

Finishing and Mounting

*W*HEN YOUR WORK *is finished, carefully check your design against the chart as it is easy to miss beads or stitches. Check that there are no loose ends at the back of the work and that all the beads and stitches are secure.*

WASHING AND PRESSING YOUR WORK

As the beads are made of glass, it is usually possible to wash your work. However, due to the manufacturing process used, they cannot be guaranteed colour-fast so do check that the colours do not run before washing your design. If the colours are fast, wash the work in warm, soapy water. Rinse, and roll in a towel to dry. When dry, lay your work face down on another thick towel, and, without distorting the lie of the beads, press it carefully on the back using a warm iron.

Neat work can be spoilt by poor mounting, so it is worth taking the trouble to produce a high quality result.

MOUNTING IN A CARD

You will need:
Three-fold card with a suitable aperture
Small piece of wadding (batting)
Double-sided tape, or clear craft glue
Sharp scissors

1 Wash your hands. Fabric and card can mark easily.

2 Open the card out flat and, with a pencil, make a small mark on the side that will be folded behind the design. (It is very easy to waste time and materials by mounting your work so that the card opens the wrong way round!)

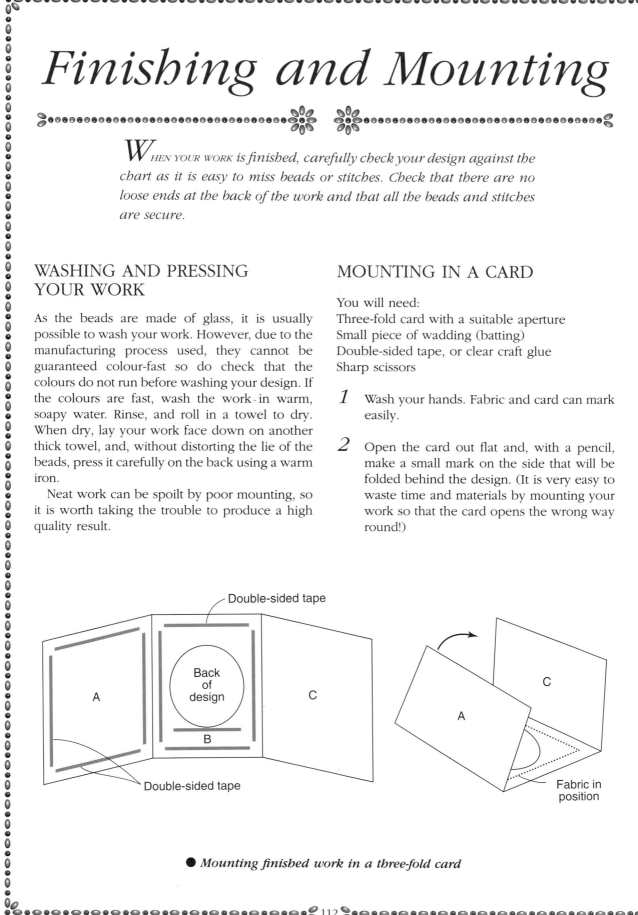

● *Mounting finished work in a three-fold card*

3 Measure and cut the double-ended tape to fit along the two sides of the card where the design will go, and then cut two pieces to fit round the aperture. If you prefer to use clear craft glue, use very small amounts so that it does not seep on to your work and out of the sides of the card when they are pressed together.

4 Trim your work to fit the aperture, leaving a margin of approximately ¼ inch (60mm) all round.

5 Using the aperture in the card as a template, carefully cut out a very thin piece of wadding (batting).

6 Remove the back of the double-sided tape around the aperture and place your work, face down, over it. Check that it is exactly as you want it and, if necessary, carefully re-position it.

7 Place the piece of wadding (batting) over the back of the design.

8 Remove the back from the rest of the double-sided tape, and carefully fold A over B.

9 Press the edges of the card together. It is now ready to add your greeting.

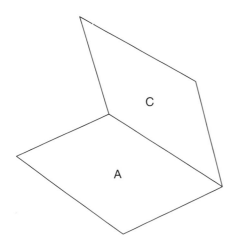

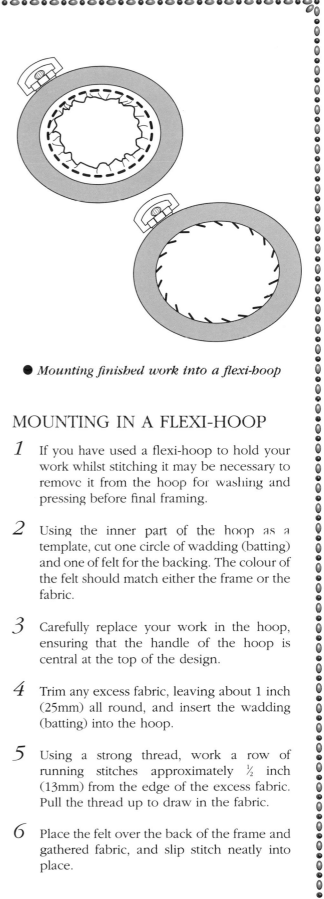

● *Mounting finished work into a flexi-hoop*

MOUNTING IN A FLEXI-HOOP

1 If you have used a flexi-hoop to hold your work whilst stitching it may be necessary to remove it from the hoop for washing and pressing before final framing.

2 Using the inner part of the hoop as a template, cut one circle of wadding (batting) and one of felt for the backing. The colour of the felt should match either the frame or the fabric.

3 Carefully replace your work in the hoop, ensuring that the handle of the hoop is central at the top of the design.

4 Trim any excess fabric, leaving about 1 inch (25mm) all round, and insert the wadding (batting) into the hoop.

5 Using a strong thread, work a row of running stitches approximately ½ inch (13mm) from the edge of the excess fabric. Pull the thread up to draw in the fabric.

6 Place the felt over the back of the frame and gathered fabric, and slip stitch neatly into place.

READY-MADE MOUNTS

Trinket boxes, trays, penholders etc come with clear mounting instructions from the manufacturers. If followed carefully, they will produce a good result. The acetate disc, supplied with small items such as boxes, will distort the lie of the beads if it is placed over them and it should be discarded or used as extra backing behind the work.

FRAMES

There are many ready-made picture frames, available through needlework shops, which are particularly suitable for smaller pieces of work and cost much less than professional framing. Photograph frames may also be used and, again, these are readily available. For a large piece of work that has already cost time and money, professional framing may, however, be the wisest choice. In this instance, you may still wish to stretch and mount the work yourself.

STRETCHING AND MOUNTING

You will need:
Acid-free mount board, available from stationers
Stanley knife
Metal ruler
Cutting board
Strong sewing thread

1 On the cutting board, cut the mount board to fit the size of frame being used (allowing extra if a window mount is to be placed inside the frame).

2 Place your work face down with the board on top. When in the correct position, fold over the edges of the fabric at the top and bottom, and pin them to the edge of the board, stretching the fabric gently. Check frequently that your work is still correctly positioned and straight.

3 Using a length of strong thread, lace back and forth over the back of the work from top to bottom. Pull up the stitches to tighten, and secure firmly.

4 Finally, lace from side to side in the same way.

Beadwork is best framed without glass as this may distort the lie of the beads when placed over them. If the work begins to look dirty, remove it from the frame, wash it (see page 112), and remount it when it is dry.

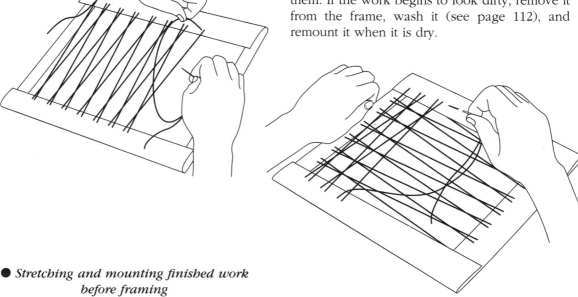

● *Stretching and mounting finished work before framing*

BEADESIGN SEED BEADS
AND MILL HILL EQUIVALENTS

BEADESIGN NO.	COLOUR	MILL HILL NO.	BEADESIGN NO.	COLOUR	MILL HILL NO.
1	Rainbow White (R)	161	13	Wine (I)	3033(CL)
2	White (P)	479			3025(CL)
3	Rainbow Pink (R)	2018			3030(CL)
4	Baby Pink (P)	145	14	Heather (Ld)	206
5	Medium Pink (P)	2005	15	Rainbow Mauve (R)	62047(F)
6	Rose Pink (P)	2004	16	Lilac (P)	151
7	Clover Pink (Matt)		17	Medium Lilac (P)	2009
8	Clover Pink	553	18	Deep Purple (I)	
9	Amethyst (SL)	3023(A)	19	Purple/Blue (Ld)	252
10	Plum (L)	2012	20	Light Blue (R)	2017
		3003(CL)	21	Light Blue (P)	143
11	Plum (C)	62056(CL)	22	Baby Blue (P)	146
12	Claret (Ld)	367	23	Mid Blue (R)	168

Index

Page numbers in *italics* indicate illustrations